HISTORIC TEXAS COURTHOUSES

BRIGHT SKY PRESS

Box 416
Albany, Texas 76430

10 9 8 7 6 5 4 3 2 1

Library of Congress Cataloging-in-Publication Data

Andrews, Michael. A., 1944–
   Historic Texas courthouses / by Michael A. Andrews.
      p. cm.
   Includes bibliographical references and index.
   ISBN-13: 978-1-931721-74-5 (alk. paper)
   ISBN-10: 1-931721-74-2 (alk. paper)
1. Historic buildings—Texas—Pictorial works. 2. Courthouses—Texas—Pictorial works. 3. Courthouses—Texas-History. 4. Texas—History, Local—Pictorial works. I. Title.

F387.A53 2006
976.4'0640222—dc22

2006040559

Photo captions:
This page: Fayette County
Page 3: Tarrant County
Page 4: Ellis County
Pages 6–7 (left to right): Shelby County, Wilson County, Parker County
Pages 8–9 (top left to right): McLennan County, Brooks County, Harrison County
Pages 10–11 (left to right): Jefferson County, Rockwall County, Young County
Page 12: Bexar County
Page 15: Fayette County
Page 17: Dallas County
Pages 18–19 (left to right): Leon County, Nueces County, Llano County
Page 21: Victoria County
Page 22: Gonzales County
Page 25: Fayette County (outside), Caldwell County (inside)
Page 27: Maverick County
Page 29: Shelby County
Page 147: Anderson County
Page 149: Stephens County (top), McLennan County (bottom)
Page 227: Jefferson County
Page 229: Travis County
Page 271: Hill County

Endsheet photography by Watt M. Casey, Jr.
Book and cover design by Isabel Lasater Hernandez
Edited by Cynthia Sellman Mendez

Printed in China through Asia Pacific Offset

Photography in *Historic Texas Courthouses* was made possible
by generous grants and contributions from the following:

Akin Gump Strauss Hauer & Feld LLP

Beirne, Maynard & Parsons LLP

Bell County Museum

Booziotis & Company Architects

Dallas Architectural Foundation

Frost Financial Management Group

Greater Houston Preservation Alliance

Litigation Section, State Bar of Texas

National Trust for Historic Preservation

Summerlee Foundation

Thompson & Knight LLP

Vinson & Elkins LLP

HISTORIC TEXAS COURTHOUSES

MICHAEL ANDREWS

PHOTOGRAPHY BY
PAUL HESTER & LISA HARDAWAY

BRIGHT SKY PRESS

CONTENTS

FOREWORD

BY RICHARD MOE

In a book published by the National Trust and the National Geographic Society a few years ago, writer and commentator Ray Suarez noted that America's historic places carry "the DNA of democracy." It's an exceptional description, and it seems to me that no other building type fits it better than the courthouses that stand in cities and towns all over our nation.

With 254 counties, Texas might be expected to have at least a few courthouses with genuine architectural significance—but in fact, the Lone Star State's collection of these landmarks is absolutely unmatched in the diversity and quality of their design. Many of them, especially those that date from what the Texas Historical Commission calls "the golden age of courthouse construction" between the 1880s and the 1920s, are visual knockouts, boasting enough towers, turrets, domes and porticoes to satisfy the most jaded building aficionado. Even those that are somewhat more subdued—like the Concho County building with its modest Italianate demeanor or the Cottle County courthouse with its deco-flavored buttresses—make a strong architectural statement that allows them to anchor and ornament their communities with both dignity and distinction.

The historic courthouses of Texas, like their counterparts all over America, are the products of an age when public buildings were designed to serve an important symbolic function. They were intended to be brick-and-stone embodiments of the stability of democratic government and the awesome majesty of The Rule of Law. Architects worked hard to make them "fitting," and to ensure that visitors would feel uplifted by the mere act of stepping inside to conduct business in their hallowed halls.

People took great pride in them—and no wonder. In a windblown, hardscrabble settlement far from the nearest city, a handsome courthouse offered evidence that the town had arrived, and suggested that its citizens were civilized people of good taste. Newspaper accounts were apt to describe a new courthouse as "a credit to the town," and townspeople usually responded to the compliment by positioning the building at the very heart of the community, in a landscaped square dotted with important monuments: a towering flagpole, a bandstand, a war memorial.

The idea that the architecture of public buildings should translate abstract ideals and values into imposing reality has largely gone out of fashion, but more than 200 historic Texas courthouses continue to play the role for which they were designed. They serve a critically important civic and judicial function, of course, but they also help give communities a sense of identity and a tangible connection with their past.

Unfortunately, as every preservationist knows, architectural and historical significance can't stop the clock. The passing decades weren't always kind to Texas courthouses, and the effects of time and hard use eventually left many of them so shabby and battered that they landed on the National Trust's list of "America's 11 Most Endangered Historic Places" in 1998. The following year, Preservation Texas and the Texas Historical Commission issued a call to action to save the state's historic courthouses. In response, then-Governor George W. Bush, with strong support from First Lady Laura Bush, and the Texas Legislature launched an unprecedented effort to prepare these beloved landmarks for new centuries of service and return them to their rightful glory as community centerpieces that are powerful—and beautiful—symbols of the Lone Star State.

The Legislature appropriated millions of dollars for the program, and millions more have come from other sources. The

results, as seen in the stunning photography by Paul Hester and Lisa Hardaway, are spectacular. Preservation plans have been prepared and approved for more than a hundred historic courthouses. Dozens of projects, from planning to emergency repairs and top-quality restoration, have received funding. More than two dozen courthouses already have been restored and rededicated, and work is underway on others. In short, the Texas Historic Courthouse Preservation Program is a rousing success—so much so that the National Trust saluted it with a National Preservation Honor Award in 2004.

One-hundred of the "best" Texas courthouses (what a tough choice that must have been!) are profiled in these pages. Author Michael Andrews not only is a distinguished former member of Congress from Texas, but also a passionate preservationist, as evidenced by his service on the board of the National Trust and his record as an articulate and effective champion of preservation on Capitol Hill. He is just the right person to tell the story of the courthouses that dot the landscape of the state he loves—and he does it here with just the right mix of scholarship and flair.

This handsome, insightful book is a reminder that Texans have a well-known, and generally well-deserved, reputation for doing things in a big way. Over the years, they built courthouses that are a big presence in county seats from Brownsville to Dalhart. When the deteriorated condition of these landmarks was recognized as a big problem, Texans created a big program to fix it. The effort got big results—and that's big news for all of us, Texans and non-Texans alike, who want to ensure a proud and productive future for the historic places that are our legacy from the past.

Richard Moe is president of the National Trust for Historic Preservation.

PUBLISHER'S NOTE:

The restoration of courthouses continues in many Texas counties. As these buildings undergo a renewal, we will update the progress—and the efforts of the Texans who love this part of their history—in future editions.

INTRODUCTION

There is no greater expression of a civilization's fundamental values and highest aspirations than its public architecture, and among the most significant and historic structures in Texas are the state's county courthouses. These magnificent governmental buildings reflect the independence and fortitude of a resolute people determined to create order and permanence out of a vast wilderness, and they are tangible evidence of a Texas history that is authentic and lasting.

Many of these architectural treasures were erected during a dramatic period of economic growth and cultural maturity. During the late nineteenth century and early twentieth century, Texas courthouses became the predominant symbol of self-government, progress and stability, and the very embodiment of a community's pride.

These buildings were not only viewed as monumental in purpose and design; they became a virtual repository of a person's life. Birth and death certificates, marriage licenses, military records, titles to property and even a rancher's brand were registered and secured at the county courthouse. The administration of public services, the holding of elections, and the assessment and collection of local taxes all took place in the county courthouse. Most importantly, Texas courthouses represented the rule of law. During the late nineteenth century, the county courthouse was the primary forum to settle disputes and uphold the laws of the state. The criminal justice system could be swift in early Texas, and in certain counties, incarceration, indictment, trial and punishment were all carried out in the same building.

The courthouse square became the focal point for celebrations, markets, parades, and innumerable civic and public functions. Memorials to a county's war heroes and most sacred causes were erected on the courthouse grounds. The courthouse became an expression of a community's character and a reflection of its worth and confidence. In some regions of the state, the courthouse was the only stone building, and in many counties, the courthouse was the tallest and most substantial structure. Visible for miles, the stately buildings became a navigation point on an empty prairie.

In early Texas, the designation as a county seat was a critical component of a community's economic development. It represented economic power, prestige and stability. The political and business leadership of a county was, in most instances, based in the county seat, and the courthouse was at the center. Highly charged elections and, at times, violence, occurred as neighboring towns competed for the coveted prize. In 1903, after a second bitter election in Hartley County, armed lawmen and cowboys from the famed XIT Ranch loaded the frame courthouse on a wagon and moved it from Hartley to Channing, near the ranch headquarters.[1]

Few governmental buildings rose in Texas during the Civil War and Reconstruction. The war and its aftermath devastated the state's mostly agricultural economy. It was not until the mid-1870s that Texas began to rebound, and it was during this period of strong economic growth—on through the turn of the century—that the grand courthouses of Texas were built.

This was a time of significant cultural maturity in Texas, and an appreciation of public architecture was sharpened as young Texas architects developed styles and design features that were consistent with more industrialized and sophisticated regions of the country. Architecture generally referred to as Victorian dominated national tastes. It included the French-influenced Second Empire style; Renaissance Revival, which included Italian and French influences; and Romanesque Revival. Community leaders strived to build

such as reinforced concrete and steel beams, enabled a fresh generation of architects to experiment with new techniques, leading to extraordinary results. More importantly, tastes changed significantly during the first three decades of the twentieth century, and the popularity of building design evolved considerably. The Classical Beaux Arts style of the early 1900s moved into a period of design that not only reflected national trends, but also was quintessentially Texan,[2] featuring Classical cruciform and Neo-Classical Revival civic buildings that were just as monumental as their predecessors. During the Roaring Twenties, the state's public buildings reflected the exuberant optimism of the day, and as in previous generations, different styles were at times blended together.

The years of the Great Depression had an enormous impact on the ability of county governments to fund the construction of new public buildings, and in most of Texas, the local tax base was severely diminished. Little new construction was even contemplated by overburdened county leaders.[3] The federal government responded to the deep economic depression with a number of aggressive New Deal programs through the Works Progress Administration and the Public Works Administration. The WPA and the PWA funded the design and construction of massive public works projects across Texas, including new public buildings. In addition, a number of Texas counties experienced economic growth because of significant oil and gas discoveries and a burgeoning energy industry. As a result, in spite of the hard economic times, a handful of Texas counties erected some of the most *important* public buildings of the period. These structures reflect the international modes of design, such as the use of the Moderne style that was highly popular during the 1930s and markedly distinctive from the past. They rank among the state's most important courthouses.

County government was the predominant form of governance in the state of Texas until the 1940s. Neither federal nor state officials affected the lives of Texans as directly as locally elected leaders, and county courthouses were the chief civic and public forums in the state.

There are 254 counties in Texas, and more than 200 of them have historic courthouses. Many of these old buildings are

public edifices that reflected their county's importance and prosperity. These buildings told a history of a small part of Texas. This was the Golden Age of Texas Courthouses.

The twentieth century brought new challenges for local political leaders, who in turn demanded a different architectural approach. Many county courthouses proved inadequate for a growing constituency, and more spatial and practical public buildings were needed. New technologies and building materials, significant architectural landmarks that have played an important role in the history of Texas. Regrettably, several courthouses have been altered over time, and as a result, have lost their essential character. Others were so poorly designed that they have little architectural significance. Sadly, fire or neglect has destroyed a number of these structures, and far too many public buildings have been razed to make room for more modern edifices. A few significant courthouses languish and decay because of a lack of restoration funds, or disinterest.

By the early 1970s, more than two dozen historic courthouses had been destroyed across the state. As a result, the Texas Legislature promulgated legislation that enacted stringent requirements regarding the demolition of these important buildings. On New Year's Day in 1993, the Hill County Courthouse in Hillsboro was ravaged by a devastating fire that gutted the once-proud building.

The destruction of the historic edifice energized preservationists and community leaders across the state. In 1998, the National Trust for Historic Preservation named the historic courthouses of Texas to its annual list of "America's 11 Most Endangered Historic Places," bringing national attention to these architectural treasures and their plight.

Then-Governor George W. Bush and the Texas Legislature vigorously responded to this challenge in 1999 by establishing the Texas Historic Courthouse Preservation Program, which provides partial matching funds to county governments for the restoration of their courthouses. The program was initially funded with a $50 million appropriation. Because of the program's success, in 2001, the Legislature approved an additional $50 million for restoration grants, and in 2003, the Legislature approved the sale of $45 million in bonds to maintain the program. The Texas Historical Commission has administered this highly successful effort with expertise, and because of its work and the commitment of local officials and preservationists, many of these important buildings have been saved and faithfully returned to their former glory.

Many are still in use today, still making history, and it is a history that is real. One can stand within their walls and hear the same sounds of history ringing through the courtrooms and hallways, or stand on the courthouse square and sense the rhythms of the past. These courthouses remain, as they were when they were built, a central stage of Texas history. The most meaningful historic buildings tell a story about their time and place, and the stories these great buildings tell us about the people who built them, the citizens who climbed their steps and entered their doors, are threads in the fabric of Texas' history.

The courthouse in Gonzales was near completion when a pardoned gunfighter and lawyer named John Wesley Hardin filed pleadings and documents in the county clerk's office that is still serving its purpose today.

The Hanging Tree on the courthouse square in Goliad still stands as citizens walk under its towering limbs.

The big second-floor courtroom in tiny Anderson, where a member of Bonnie and Clyde's gang was convicted and sentenced to death, is still called to order every week by a district judge.

The seven-hundred-pound courthouse bell in Fort Davis still chimes today, just as it did almost a hundred years ago to warn of attacks by Pancho Villa's army from across the Rio Grande.

In Cherokee and Shelby counties, politicians still draw crowds to the same courthouse squares used by Sam Houston and Lyndon Johnson in their campaigns for public office.

In Ozona, the old oak tree under which Crockett County officials erected a tent to hold their first court session in 1891 still stands near the county's courthouse, built in 1902.

The best historic architecture defines a place and connects each generation with its past. The historic courthouses of Texas form part of the framework of Texas history. These buildings are important, and their preservation and restoration is one of the great civic responsibilities of our time. It is not my intent to include every historic courthouse in this book. My purpose is to focus on 100 of the best examples of historic courthouses in Texas, and what these magnificent structures tell us about what happened there.

THE TEXAS COUNTY

Karnes County was known as "Bad Man's Paradise," and the county seat of Helena was one of the toughest towns in South Texas, where men carried pistols and jailed prisoners were held in cages near the two-room courthouse on the courthouse square. The dirty little town consisted of a group of frame buildings surrounding a small stucco courthouse. Emmett Butler was the twenty-year-old son of Colonel William Butler, the wealthiest and largest land owner in Karnes County. On the day after Christmas in 1884, he was drinking heavily in one of Helena's many bars bordering the courthouse square. It was not a surprise that the young man picked a fight with another customer. When the sheriff arrived, he brought a posse and quickly relieved him of his Winchester. A crowd formed, and when the sheriff turned, the young cowboy pulled a six-shooter hidden under his raincoat and shot the sheriff through his heart. As he died he cried, "He has shot me. Shoot him." Butler ran to his horse, and as he tried to get away, forty shots rang out, killing him and his horse.

Colonel Butler buried his son two days later, and that night he rode into town with twenty-five heavily armed men. In a driving rain, he rode around the courthouse square waving a rifle over his head: "I want the men who killed my son!" The streets were deserted, and his voice echoed against the closed buildings. No one stepped forward. "Alright then, I'll kill the town that killed my son!" Butler did kill the town. When a rail line across the county was proposed two years later, he offered the San Antonio and Aransas Pass Railway a right-of-way across his ranch. The new railroad bypassed Helena, and the county seat was moved six miles to the new town of Karnes City. Not much is left of Old Helena, only the vacant courthouse and an empty square.[4]

Town planning and the organization of counties in Texas have been largely influenced by two traditions: The Spanish and Mexican cultures, especially in South Texas, and the Anglo-American heritage of early settlers during the colonization period. Each group brought deeply ingrained disciplines to Texas and profoundly influenced the organization of towns and local governments. The courthouse square and the county seat, from the earliest days of settlement in Texas, became the central focus of civic activity, economic growth and a symbol of a community's values.[5] A vibrant town square was essential to the development of a community, and the designation as a county seat was an indicator of prosperity and leadership.

Hispanic traditions and practices brought to the New World from Spain were largely adopted by Mexico when it gained its independence in 1824.[6] The Mexican government precisely prescribed land-use requirements for new towns. Squares were central to every community, and by law, colonists were instructed how to organize their towns. Churches were given a prominent place on the town square in every new town, evidencing the strong influence of Catholicism. A site for a municipal government building was selected, as were sites for schools, a jail, public markets and a cemetery.[7] For the most part, these decisions were made not by the town's inhabitants, but by the government in Mexico City. The more populated and geographically important early towns like San Antonio strictly adhered to these rules and today retain their original street plans, plazas and squares from the eighteenth century.

During the early 1800s, Mexican authorities attempted to place a number of the most basic government functions under local control. Administering municipal ordinances from Mexico City had become impracticable, and Texas was divided into three

departments, each with strategically located townships. Within the departments of Nacogdoches, Brazos and Bexar, municipalities were strictly organized and governed by Mexican law,[8] although these townships were granted some control over basic municipal affairs. Municipalities were ruled by elected councils and a mayor, while other offices, such as sheriff, were appointed positions. Such rigid framework for governance and town planning maintained order and predictability.

Early Anglo-Americans in Texas had their own attitudes about local government. Self-rule, decentralization and a democratic form of representation modeled after the American experience were the primary causes of the Texas Revolution. These principles were reflected in the Texas Declaration of Independence and the Constitution of 1836. The new Republic of Texas established a court system that included a supreme court, county courts and justices of the peace. The right to a trial by jury, prohibited by the Mexican government, was granted along with the election of magistrates. These local governments were empowered to provide for a county's public buildings, including a courthouse and jail.[9]

The population of Texas exploded after hostilities with Mexico ceased in the spring of 1836, then estimated at 25,000. In 1850, five years after Texas entered the Union, the population of free citizens had risen to more than 215,000.[10] Partly in response to the rapidly changing demographics, the Texas Congress granted itself authority to create new counties and rules for their organization. It was a regimented process that required a petition of one hundred or more free male citizens from an area of at least nine hundred square miles. Twenty-three towns that existed in Texas at the time of the revolution were recognized by the new republic as counties. County seats could be selected by popular election of the county's citizens, the Texas Congress or the county commissioners.[11] New towns were incorporated rapidly as the population grew.

While a charter was required from the government to incorporate a city, there were no restrictions on town planning. Entrepreneurial spirit surged as business leaders and land speculators rushed to create town sites and new villages. Many of these early communities have vanished. At the advent of the Civil War in 1861, two of the more influential cities in Texas were neighboring Independence and Washington, and today, there is little evidence of either town's former size or prominence. The competition between city leaders for new businesses and citizens was spirited, and having the designation as the county seat was an important trophy. A county courthouse carried enormous political, economic and symbolic importance.

One of the most important economic factors during this period was the rapid development of railroads in Texas. Towns were created or abandoned almost overnight, depending on where the rail lines were laid. The coming of a railroad was a significant event in the life of a community. In 1928, when the first train entered the small town of Throckmorton, some 15,000 people came to stand by the courthouse and welcome its arrival. A day-long celebration included a barbecue with twenty-nine head of beef, a horse race and the reenactment of a buffalo hunt staged by Native Americans brought in from a reservation just for the occasion.[12]

The introduction of railroads produced not only economic promise, but cultural advantages as well. New technologies, the current fashions and information were carried on the rails to the far corners of Texas. For many isolated regions, the railroad was a tangible connection to the commercial centers of the state and beyond.[13] In 1887, when the first train entered Hallettsville, the town's newspaper proudly headlined: "The Iron Horse is here— Hallettsville linked with the world."[14]

Public squares date to the earliest American colonies, especially in the Mid-Atlantic and Southern states. This Anglo-American tradition complemented the Hispanic cultural experience. New towns were, in most instances, laid out in a traditional rectangular grid, and a public square was central to this arrangement. The one-block square with commercial buildings on each of the four sides was the most common arrangement, and the courthouse generally had four entrances, one facing each street of the square. Topographical or economic considerations made some modifications necessary. The town square of Fort

Worth and its courthouse were placed on a high bluff overlooking the Trinity River. In Houston, the town square and courthouse were placed near Buffalo Bayou, rather than the center of town, because that was the site of the city's primary commerce. In many instances, the town square and public buildings were placed close to the rail line rather than at the town center. Some grids were used repeatedly, and most featured the design of a rectangular block surrounded by streets and buildings.[15] The town square, from its earliest beginnings in Texas, was placed at the heart of a town—destined to become the focal point of the community.[16]

In 1876, at the end of Reconstruction, a new state constitution allowed for the creation of new counties as the population grew in the western regions of the state. It also provided new rules for designating county seats, and the requirements were specific. A proposal to create any new county had to pass both the House and Senate of the Legislature by a two-thirds vote. A new county could contain no fewer than 900 square miles in a square form,

unless previous boundary lines prevented it, or 700 square miles if created from an existing county.

The new law required that no new county seat could be created more than five miles from the center of a county. As importantly, an existing county seat could only be moved from the county's center by a vote of two-thirds of the populace, although only a simple majority was necessary to move a seat to a location within five miles of the center of the county.[17] These changes, in some cases, created highly charged elections as communities fought to have their town designated the county seat.

In 1877, a bitter campaign and election was held in Van Zandt County for relocating the county seat to Wills Point from Canton. Wills Point was declared the winner, but only after the returns were allegedly destroyed. When the county commissioners ordered the county records moved to the new county seat, 500 armed men rode into Wills Point to bring them back. The "Wills Point War" ended only after the governor sent lawmen into the county to restore order.[18]

THE GOLDEN AGE
OF TEXAS COURTHOUSES

Alfred Giles had grown accustomed to the dusty stagecoach ride, a part of the journey from his 13,000-acre ranch named Hillingdon near Comfort, to one of the many courthouses he had designed. The travel had become routine, and it gave him time to think. By 1885, he had parlayed his creative talent, his keen business sense and his family inheritance into great wealth and social standing in San Antonio. He was at the top of his career and widely recognized as one of a handful of outstanding young Texas architects. He had designed magnificent homes for some of the wealthiest families in the state, and his public buildings reflected a unique style that was sophisticated and a testament to the state's maturity.

Giles was an exact and careful man. In order to stay in touch with his wife, on each trip he took two carrier pigeons, one to release when he arrived safely and one when he started his journey home. But Giles' pigeons did him little good when masked outlaws stopped the stage with their guns drawn. The bandits forced Giles to help them collect the money and valuables from the stagecoach before they made their escape, leaving him terrified and thankful to be alive. It was a reminder to this very civilized man that Texas was still a dangerous place.[19]

In early Texas, public buildings were strictly utilitarian and simple, made from rough-hewn logs and without ornamentation. They were, in most respects, indistinguishable from the other buildings in the community. These indigenous structures were replaced with modest wooden frame buildings as the region became more populated and stable. It is not surprising that in 1836, the framers of the Texas Declaration of Independence met in a crude wooden building at Washington-on-the-Brazos.[20] In most areas of the new republic there were few carpenters and tradesmen, and little public interest in funding the construction of more permanent buildings.

Once the threat of Mexican invasion eased, there was a movement to build public buildings that reflected the new nation's aspirations and addressed the increasing needs for security and space. These designs were greatly influenced by the courthouses of the South. Many of the settlers had migrated from the Mid-Atlantic regions of the country and brought with them a common cultural heritage. Greek Revival architecture was popular across the country, especially in the South, and many of these relatively small, square buildings had only two floors and one large courtroom. They were uncomplicated in design and most were of wooden-frame construction. Only a small number were constructed of bricks or stone. In many regions of the state, a stone courthouse was the only non-wooden structure, which added to its significance. These sturdy buildings resembled courthouses in Virginia and other Southern states, which was an important symbol for Texans intent on bringing sophistication and tradition to their communities.[21]

Texas grew more prosperous in the years leading up to the Civil War, and more elaborate and sophisticated public buildings were built. These buildings were more substantial and durable than their predecessors. In addition, building materials became more varied, and most new buildings were built of masonry. Exterior ornamentation became more common during the antebellum period, and cupolas, clocks, bell towers and porticoes were frequently used.

The Civil War and Reconstruction stalled the construction of courthouses across the state. Many were remodeled, and new ones

were generally constructed in proportion and style to their antebellum predecessors. It was one of the worst economic periods in Texas history, and the civic architecture reflected the hard times.

In the mid-1870s, the Texas economy rebounded substantially, and the state enjoyed a time of unparalleled economic growth and expansion that lasted into the twentieth century. With a rapidly expanding tax base, county leadership could consider ambitious plans for new public buildings that would reflect a community's prosperity and advancement from the dark days of the war and Reconstruction. There was no better way to express this growing optimism than by erecting new and more spatial courthouses. In 1881, the Texas Legislature encouraged the construction of courthouses by promulgating a law enabling counties to issue bonds for their financing. As a result, almost every county in the state built a new courthouse.[22] It was during this robust period of Texas history that several of the state's most treasured examples of architecture were created.

During the latter part of the nineteenth century, most American architects faithfully followed designs and methods popular in Europe. Victorian styles were emulated throughout the United States and took several forms as designs were created to respond to unique challenges in different regions of the country. During the last quarter of the century, tastes evolved and courthouses from county to county reflected those differences. Italianate, Second Empire, Victorian Gothic and Queen Anne modes of design were all employed, at times independently. In many instances, various elements of different styles were combined in the same building. It is partly for this reason that the style of Henry Hobson Richardson had such an important influence on Texas courthouse construction.

At the close of the nineteenth century, Richardson stood alone as the most celebrated and accomplished living architect in America. His work was unsurpassed in its brilliance and beauty.[23] Richardson singularly changed the face of design from its European predominance and set a new standard that was quintessentially American. He is the only American architect of his time to have influenced modes of design in Europe.[24] In 1885, one year before his death, in a poll of the ten best buildings in America, Richardson's work took up half the list.[25] His design for Trinity Church in Boston made him famous; the church is still considered one of the nation's most beautiful buildings. Its elements have been copied across the country in every type of public architecture.[26] The Richardson Romanesque was the perfect embodiment of a changing nation, and his sense of design and composition perfectly suited America's Gilded Age.

Richardson was a behemoth of a man, weighing well over three-hundred pounds with an equally expansive charm. He became a celebrity and joined other luminaries of his day—Henry Adams, Emily Dickinson and Mark Twain—at the pinnacle of the cultural and artistic elite in America. He never traveled to Texas, and he was never commissioned to design a building in the state. But his influence over a generation of young Texas architects was profound. His use of natural materials and monumental proportions was well-suited for Texas, and during the 1890s, Richardson Romanesque courthouses were scattered across the state.

The best Texas architects of the nineteenth century left an indelible mark on the state, and the courthouses they designed framed an important era of Texas history. Sources of information are surprisingly scarce about a group of designers who left such grand and enduring monuments across the state's landscape. Wesley Clark Dodson fought for the Confederacy and traveled to Texas from Alabama, settling first in Galveston and later Waco.[27] Eugene T. Heiner of Indiana became the first prominent architect in Houston.[28] Nicholas J. Clayton was raised in Ohio, fought for the Union during the Civil War and settled in Galveston.[29] The brothers Frederick and Oscar Ruffini were raised in a strong German community in Cleveland, Ohio, and established their practice in Austin, although later Oscar relocated to San Angelo.[30] James E. Flanders was reared and trained in Chicago and practiced his craft in Dallas.[31] Alonzo Dawson was born in Hartford, Connecticut, and had a widely successful practice in Texas that spanned twenty-five years. Dawson worked first in Fort Worth and later in Houston.[32]

These architects were varied in their background and training, and each brought different skills to compete with one another in designing the public buildings of their day. Most were not well-traveled and many were isolated from the mainstream of national trends and practices with little formal education in design and architecture. They all were trained in an apprenticeship system and generally worked independently in small offices. They competed with one another for commissions and against builders for contracts. Master architect Nicholas J. Clayton, famous for the impressive buildings he designed in Galveston,[33] worked assiduously to establish architecture as a professional discipline in late nineteenth century Texas.[34] Clayton's magnificent 1898 Galveston County Courthouse survived the 1900 hurricane, but not the county leaders who destroyed it in 1965 to build a more modern building.

Gordon[35] and Alfred Giles[36] were two of the most prominent and certainly the most well-known Texas architects of their day. James Riely Gordon was one of Richardson's most faithful followers.[37] He was born in Winchester, Virginia, in 1863 and moved to San Antonio in 1874. During his career, he designed seventeen courthouses that were constructed in Texas. Several that are still standing today include buildings in Bexar, Comal, Ellis, Erath, Fayette, Gonzales, Hopkins, Lee, Victoria, Wise, McLennan and Harrison counties. These grand buildings are exceptional, and they all were designed with varying degrees of the Richardson Romanesque style.[38] Gordon's dramatic courthouse presentation sketches and renderings included spacious veranda and roof gardens adorned with "beautiful Texas foliage" in order to suggest a "Spanish vista."[39] The master architect had an exceptional sense of theater, designing his large courtrooms as a stage with the judge's bench elevated above the proceedings for dramatic effect.[40]

Unlike many of his contemporaries, Gordon was not limited in his career experiences. He worked as a supervising architect of the United States Treasury in Washington, D.C. He initially studied architecture with two established Texas architects, J.N. Preston and W.K. Dobson in San Antonio. He opened his practice first in San Antonio and later moved it to Dallas, designing hundreds of private and public buildings in the state. Gordon was a leader in improving the professionalism of his craft, successfully leading an effort before the Legislature to require licensing and standards for the practice, and he was an original founder of the Texas State Association of Architects.[41] He enjoyed a national reputation, and in 1902, moved to New York where his practice prospered. He was honored by his colleagues and served thirteen years as president of the New York Society of Architects. Gordon is credited with designing sixty-nine courthouses before his death in 1937.[42]

Alfred Giles was born in 1853 on his family estate near London. He attended the best private schools in England and studied the arts at King's College in London. At seventeen, he apprenticed at an established architectural firm. In 1873, Giles settled in New York to start his career. Largely for health reasons, he moved to San Antonio because of the region's drier climate. Like many young architects, he worked for a contractor before starting his own firm in 1876, just as the post-Reconstruction economy in Texas began to boom.[43]

San Antonio was the center of Giles' professional and personal world. He garnered commissions from the city's wealthiest families, and, like many of his clients, he became a civic and cultural leader. He was prolific, designing more than twenty buildings for one family alone, and more than forty commercial and private residences in San Antonio.[44] Giles was an astute businessman and became one of the most successful and progressive ranchers in Texas.

Giles' style was eclectic. Most of his public buildings are noteworthy for their simplicity and understatement. He was a man of taste and refinement, and his courthouses reflected his sense of symmetry and art.

The courthouses of the Golden Age are among the most important historical structures in the state. At no other time in Texas history has public architecture so clearly defined an era. Many of the elegant and monumental buildings that remain still dominate and symbolize their communities today, just as they did when their doors first opened.

GILLESPIE COUNTY

GILLESPIE COUNTY COURTHOUSE

Fredericksburg. 1881
Alfred Giles. Architect

In 1881, the Gillespie County Commissioners placed advertisements in San Antonio and Austin newspapers inviting bids to design a new courthouse, with a prize of fifty dollars to the winning architect. F.E. Ruffini and Alfred Giles both submitted plans and the commissioners voted unanimously in favor of Giles. The gracious winner asked that the fifty dollars be given to Ruffini for his expenses. Giles' careful specifications for the building contractors would be a hallmark of his work: "Sand used in the masonry was to be well-screened, sharp, and free from soil and vegetable matter. Three parts of sand and part of freshly burnt lime were to compound the mortar. The cement formula was one part of Rosendale to two parts of sand. Foundations were to be of flat rocks, laid in half and through courses, while construction of the walls was to be of hammer-dressed rustic rubble in half, third and through bonds."[45]

This 1882 Renaissance Revival courthouse for Gillespie County sits on the main square of Fredericksburg and now serves as a public library. It is a beautiful example of the early work of Alfred Giles and was restored by community leaders in 1967. Well-proportioned, the old courthouse features light yellow and white limestone from nearby quarries. The fine details of the cast iron cornices and brackets that support the standing-seam tin roof are exemplary. Tall double-hung windows enhance the building's appearance. The locks and doorknobs display an engraved hummingbird design, etched in copper.

Many of the original benches, tables and stand-up desks, all made by area craftsmen, have been carefully preserved and remain in use.

SHACKELFORD COUNTY COURTHOUSE

Albany. 1883
James Edward Flanders. Architect

On June 22, 1883, "The Albany Star" reported: "The Old Courthouse is gone. Charley Hatfield moved it away last Wednesday to the rear of his restaurant and we are informed that he purposes to use it for lodging rooms for parties working on the courthouse."

On June 21, 1883, "The Albany Echo" reported: "Be it remembered that on Thursday, June 21, 1883, the first stone was dressed and the first shovel full of earth removed for the foundation of the new courthouse! ... Within twenty-four hours after their bond was approved they had men quarrying stone, teams hauling and cutters dressing.... Hurrah for the new courthouse!"[46]

Designed by Dallas architect James E. Flanders, this elegant Second Empire courthouse with strong Italianate elements is one of the best examples of the highly decorative style. The golden-colored sandstone was quarried from a ranch a short distance from Albany.

Five chimneys and more than a dozen stoves kept the courthouse warm. Each section of the copper roof has a narrow catwalk braced by ornamental iron cresting. The clock tower bell was hung in 1898 and has a clapper for ringing and a striker for tolling, which is still used for funerals.

Carefully preserved by the people of Albany, this proud edifice of justice dominates the town and the surrounding  ranchland, much as it did in the late nineteenth century. The building was the first participant in the Texas Historic Courthouse Preservation Program, and was restored and rededicated in 2001.

The rough-faced ashlar walls contrast nicely with the smooth-faced quoins and dressed stringcourses that encircle the building. Unlike many Victorian styled courthouses of the era, the windows are not high-reaching and the ornamentation is measured.

Flanders was a successful and popular architect in West Texas, where he would design at least ten courthouses. His courthouse in Albany is the only one that remains.[47]

LAMPASAS COUNTY COURTHOUSE

Lampasas. 1883
Wesley Clark Dodson. Architect

"I didn't kill all of them men—but then again, I got some that wasn't on the bill, so I guess it just about evens up."—Pink Higgins

In 1876, Pink Higgins was a Lampasas cattleman and trail driver. Higgins knew the Horrell brothers to be cattle thieves and murderers, and when he was sure they were rustling from his herd, he confronted them in the Gem Saloon near the courthouse. Higgins quickly drew his pistol and killed Merritt Horrell. The Horrell brothers were enraged by the shooting and quick to seek revenge. When they were ambushed on the road to Lampasas, a Texas Ranger went after Pink Higgins. The rancher surrendered and was ordered to appear in court. Shortly before his hearing date, the district clerk's office in the courthouse was burglarized and the records were destroyed. Three days later, both sides met on the courthouse square and shot it out. A man from each side was killed. The violence was enough for the citizens of Lampasas. This time a company of Texas Rangers arrived, arrested the Horrell brothers and negotiated a peace agreement. The Horrell family and Pink Higgins were forced by the Rangers to execute letters of reconciliation ending the bloodshed.[48]

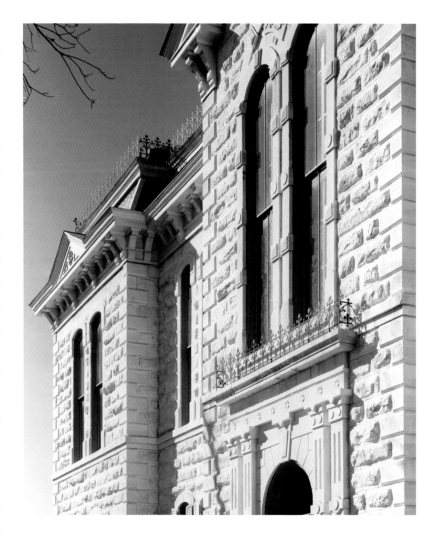

The Lampasas Courthouse features Second Empire and Italianate styles of architecture. It has a sheet metal convex mansard roof and a bell tower, topped with a deck. The tin shingles that cover the bell tower and mansard roof are placed in a diamond pattern. The original roof was made of black slate. After the original plans by W.C. Dodson were approved, the county commissioners authorized a four-faced Seth Thomas clock to be placed in the central tower. The exterior walls are of native limestone quarried near Lampasas.

The first courthouse for Lampasas County burned on Christmas Eve in 1871. The county records that were not destroyed in the fire were lost in the raging flood waters of the Lampasas River. This is the second courthouse for the county and one of the oldest Texas courthouses still in use by a county government. County leaders elected to participate in the Texas Historic Courthouse Preservation Program, and the building was restored to its 1883 condition and rededicated in 2004.[49]

BELL COUNTY COURTHOUSE

Belton. 1884

Jasper Newton Preston & Sons. Architects

I n 1848, settlers along the Leon River petitioned the Legislature for the right to create a new county to be called Clear Water. The following year, the Legislature responded by creating three new counties along the Balcones Escarpment north of Austin. The organization of the county government took place under the "Charter Oak," and court proceedings were held at a blacksmith shop until 1851, when the first courthouse was built in the new county seat of Belton. The Legislature named Belton and Bell County after their new governor, Peter Hansborough Bell. Bell is one of the forgotten historical leaders of Texas. He joined Sam Houston's army as a private and fought at San Jacinto and later became a captain in the Texas Rangers. During the war with Mexico, Bell won praise for his valor at the Battle of Buena Vista. During the Civil War, he was a colonel in the Confederate Army. Bell was twice-elected governor and served four years in the U.S. Congress.[50]

This stately Renaissance Revival temple of justice more closely resembles a state capitol than a seat of local government. The building's most distinguished characteristic is its grand clock tower with a columned gallery, which rises 125 feet. The exterior walls of the first floor are of rusticated limestone, with smooth stonework above. The golden-hued limestone was from a local quarry. The imposing building features four porticoed facades

that open to each side of the county square, round-arched windows and arched passageways. A watchful Statue of Justice with the scales of justice and sword in hand graces the building's monumental proportions.

An impressive statue of Governor Peter H. Bell, the county's namesake and third governor of Texas, stands at one corner of the courthouse square.

This is the third courthouse for Bell County. In 1950, county leaders decided to modernize the building and made extensive changes, including removing the clock tower. In 1999, county leaders and preservationists rebuilt the tower and returned the exterior of the building to its original grandeur.

WILSON COUNTY COURTHOUSE

Floresville. 1884
Alfred Giles. Architect

During Reconstruction, the military government that ruled Texas appointed judges and clerks for each county. In Wilson County, carpetbag Judge John W. Longsworth held both positions, and in 1867, he arbitrarily ordered the county seat moved from Sutherland Springs to Lodi, when local citizens allegedly refused to pay him a fee. After Reconstruction, it was moved back to Sutherland Springs in March of 1871, and four months later, it was moved again to Lodi. In 1873, an election was held, and the new town of Floresville, located near the center of the county, was chosen as the county seat. A few months after the election, the courthouse mysteriously burned, and the citizens of Sutherland Springs quickly petitioned for another election. In 1883, Floresville won again by a margin of 250 votes.[51]

Floresville is located on the upper coastal plain of South Texas. In 1883, Wilson County political leaders commissioned Alfred Giles to design a new courthouse to replace the wooden frame building that had been destroyed by fire. The result was an exceptional brick Italianate structure framed with stone quoins, stringcourses and metal cornices. The brick walls were stuccoed in the 1930s.

The prominent pyramidal tower rises above the small town of Floresville, and the Goddess of Justice, holding a sword of truth and the scales of justice, prominently stands watch over all those who enter.

RED RIVER COUNTY COURTHOUSE

Clarksville. 1884

William H. Wilson. Architect

In 1841, the attacks by marauding bands of Indians had become a crisis for the new republic, and twenty frontier counties, including Red River County, were authorized by the Texas Congress to raise volunteer companies of Mounted Minute Men to protect the settlements. The companies were organized in each county seat and elected their own captain. The volunteers were required at all times to be "prepared with a good substantial horse, bridle and saddle, with other necessary accoutrements, together with a good gun, and one-hundred rounds of ammunition ...." The Mounted Minute Men were made exempt from "paying a state, county, or corporation poll tax, and the tax assessed by law upon one horse." [52]

Dallas architect William H. Wilson utilized a Classical design that features variations of Renaissance Revival and Second Empire architecture. The large tower supports a four-faced clock with dials that are eight and one-half feet in diameter, and a two-thousand-pound bell. The unique ocher-colored stone used for the outer walls is from a quarry at the nearby town of Honey Grove. An annex was attached to the building in 1910.

When layers of old paint were removed from the interior walls during the structure's restoration, an elaborate Victorian paint scheme was uncovered, including a stenciled phrase "Thou Shalt Not Bear Witness" behind the judge's bench. [53]

The Red River County Courthouse is one of the oldest in the state that is still in use. As a participant in the Texas Historic Courthouse Preservation Program, this remarkable building was faithfully restored and rededicated in 2002.

The columns and pedestals project from the corners of the building, which was a unique feature for a public building in nineteenth century Texas. A distinctive bracketed cornice topped by decorative metal cresting frames the impressive structure.

The base of the building is of rock-faced ashlar and the walls are made with cut stones with flat hammered faces and smooth margins, which are marked by prominent stringcourses.

SHELBY COUNTY COURTHOUSE

Center. 1885

John Joseph Emmett Gibson. Architect/Builder

In the summer of 1948, Coke Stevenson was the most popular Texas politician since Sam Houston. He had served as speaker, lieutenant governor and governor of Texas longer than anyone in the history of the state. He was fondly known as "Mr. Texas," especially in East Texas, where his conservative base ran deep. Coke Stevenson was invincible, and no one thought his opponent for an open U.S. Senate seat in the Democratic primary run-off had much of a chance, but a young congressman from the Hill Country had a plan.

Lyndon Johnson started his campaign for the Senate in front of the Shelby County Courthouse in Center, the heart of Stevenson's political support. Johnson's friends put up signs around the county, placed advertisements in the local newspapers and on the radio inviting Shelby County voters to the event, and they came. Hundreds stood on the lawn; some leaned against the Confederate memorial; and others listened from their cars or through the open windows of the old courthouse. Johnson had a microphone strapped to his chest so he could walk around, wave both hands and get close to the crowd when he spoke. He repeated the speech on courthouse squares across the state, and when the votes were counted, Johnson won by 87 votes, the closest Senate race in Texas history.[54]

After a fire destroyed the wooden courthouse and jail in 1882, county leaders commissioned John Joseph Emmett Gibson, an  Irish immigrant, to design and build a new structure. The result was a weighty Gothic courthouse in the style of an ancient Irish castle. Gibson combined rounded turrets, heavy buttresses and decorative brickwork to

form a structure that still dominates its environment. The red and gray bricks were made at the architect's own kiln, and most of the building materials were acquired locally.

The large second-floor courtroom is impressive with its finely crafted woodwork and decorative trusses and braces. Behind the judicial bench is an "escape hatch" enabling the judge to climb down a flight of hidden stairs that leads to a back door in the building.

Gibson designed and built an almost identical courthouse in 1885 for neighboring Panola County, which county leaders destroyed in 1953 to build a modern building. In 2000, leaders in Shelby County completed the restoration of their courthouse, which now serves as a museum.

MAVERICK COUNTY COURTHOUSE

Eagle Pass. 1885

James W. Wahrenberger and Alfred F. Beckman. Architects

I n 1889, when Maverick County officials found the remains of three women and a young boy weighted with rocks in the Rio Grande, they petitioned the Texas Rangers to investigate. On a tip from a cowboy named Picnic Jones, the lawmen tracked the killer to San Saba. Dan Duncan was indicted for the brutal murders and was tried, convicted and sentenced to death by Judge Winchester Kelso in the second-story courtroom of the Maverick County Courthouse. The defendant's trial and unsuccessful appeals brought national attention to Eagle Pass. He was hanged in the county jail in 1891, the county's only capital execution.[55]

Located in southwest Texas along the Rio Grande, Eagle Pass was named the county seat when Maverick County was established in 1856. The town sits along the historic El Camino Real, which for centuries was the main roadway from Monterrey, Mexico, to Louisiana.

By 1884, a new railroad crossing over the Rio Grande and a new toll bridge had increased commercial activity and brought new citizens to the isolated border town. The temporary quarters that were used for court proceedings had proven inadequate, and county leaders commissioned the construction of a permanent courthouse and jail, which were completed the following year.

This Romanesque Revival brick structure with its Second Empire influences resembles a Spanish fortress or an early government building in Mexico City. It is a beautifully appropriate structure for the bicultural county seat.

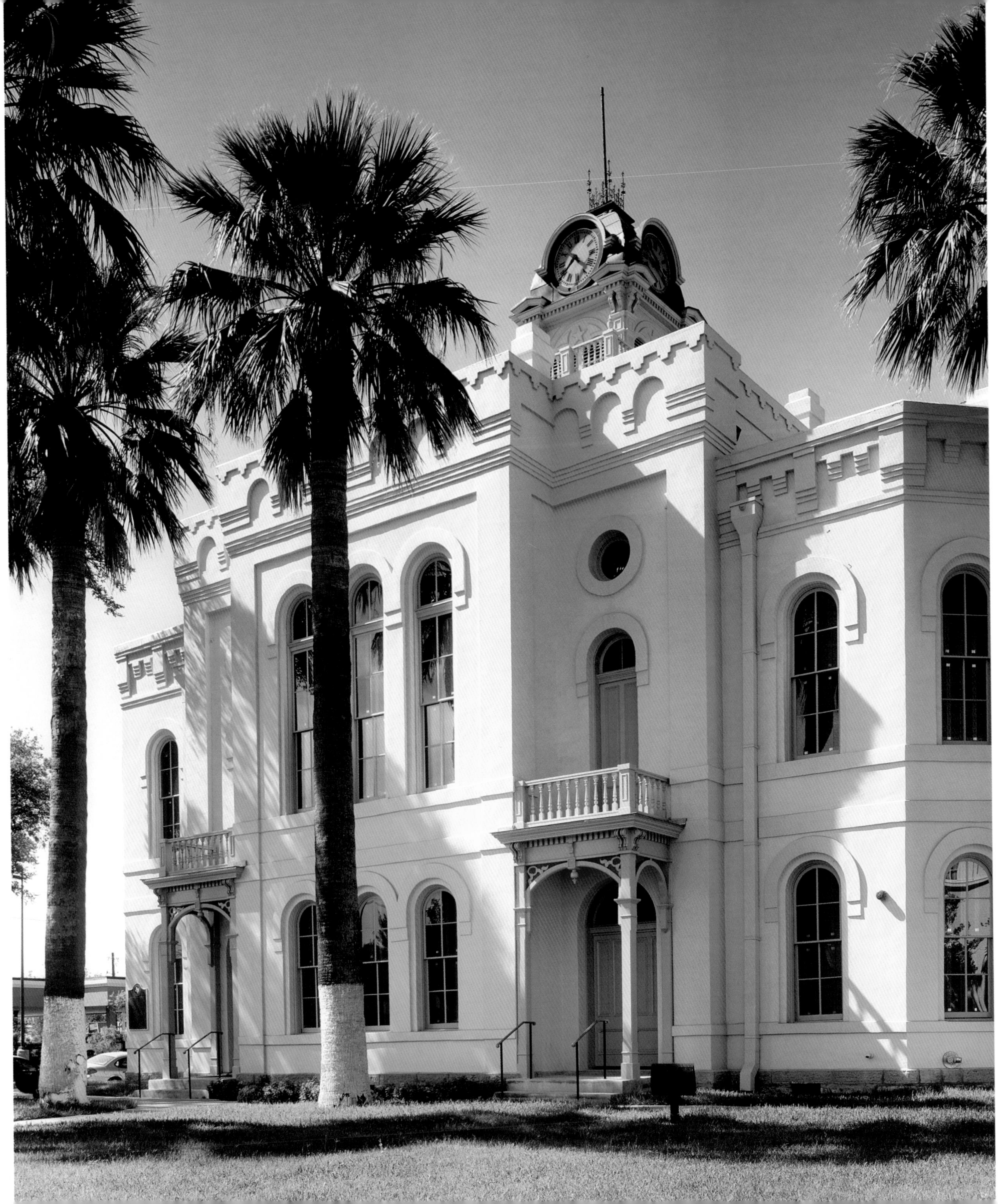

During the repair and restoration, a colorful Mexican Art Nouveau decorative paint scheme was uncovered in the building's interior. Detailed patterns in cream and ocher colors on the first floor complement the exterior colors, which are reminiscent of the region. On the walls of the second-floor courtroom, stenciled patterns of gray flowered pendants on blue walls were discovered beneath coats of paint. The paint scheme has been faithfully restored to its original beauty.[56]

Roman arched windows and dominant stringcourses add decoration to the brick structure. The tall windows on the second story bring light to the large courtroom. A picturesque clock tower rises from the parapet. The four-sided clock still operates with its original works and bell. The treasured Maverick County Courthouse has undergone a complete interior and exterior restoration, returning it to its 1885 appearance. The palm tree-shaded courthouse was rededicated by county leaders in 2005.

PARKER COUNTY COURTHOUSE

Weatherford. 1886
Wesley Clark Dodson and Dudley. Architects

I n 1814, at the Battle of Horse Shoe Bend, Isaac Parker and Sam Houston fought side by side under the command of General Andrew Jackson. They became friends for life. In 1833, Parker moved to Texas with his wife and thirty-two members of his family and settled in the town of Mustang Prairie, where they built a fort for protection against the Indians. During the Texas Revolution, Parker joined Elisha Clapp's company of rangers. While Parker was away, a band of 500 Kiowa and Comanche Indians attacked the stockade, slaughtered many of his family members and captured his niece and nephew, Cynthia Ann and John Parker. When Texas became a republic, Parker served in the Texas Congress and later as a state representative after Texas was admitted to the Union. At the age of 67, a widowed Parker joined the Confederate army with his 40-year-old son. After the war, he remarried and at the age of 84, became the father of his youngest child. He died in 1883 and is buried near Weatherford by the side of one of his sons in the county that bears his name.[57]

The first district court for Parker County was held in a post oak grove by the side of the Fort Worth and Fort Belknap Stage Road until a courthouse was completed in 1856.[58] This is an excellent Second Empire limestone building designed by the firm of Dodson and Dudley. It is the fourth courthouse for the county. W.C. Dodson was a prolific and popular architect of courthouses in the 1880s. His

courthouse for Parker County was one of several in which he incorporated the same themes. Courthouses for Lampasas, Hill and Hood counties also were designed by Dodson, and while their similarities are striking, he incorpo- rated subtle changes based on the available building materials, county budgets and his own sense of proportion and style.

The tall bell tower and corner pavilions with mansard roofs are characteristic of Dodson's architectural style.

A participant in the Texas Historic Courthouse Preservation Program, the elegant building was restored in 2003 and rededicated in 2005. The second-floor district courtroom, one of the largest in the state, was restored to its original size. The courtroom's decorative wall and ceiling paint, small wooden balconies and patterned floor coverings also have been restored. The towering building dominates the town center. Over the years the courthouse square has been paved with parking lots and roadways, and local community leaders hope to restore the square to its original landscaped design.

CONCHO COUNTY COURTHOUSE

Paint Rock. 1886
F.E. Ruffini. Architect

In 1879, when ranchers along the Concho River petitioned the Legislature to form a new county, there were fewer than a hundred people living on the rugged open range not far from where the Concho joined the Red Fork of the Colorado River. There were no settlements or towns in the new county, so the cattlemen chose a well-traveled ford on the Concho near Kickapoo Creek for a county seat and named it Paint Rock, after the ancient Indian pictographs on nearby bluffs.[59] By 1886, when the new courthouse opened for business, there were only 100 people living in Paint Rock. Today, the county seat has fewer than 300 residents.

Brothers Oscar and F.E. Ruffini sometimes collaborated on projects, but often worked alone to design the Second Empire courthouses they became known for across West Texas. F.E. Ruffini died soon after he designed this carefully crafted courthouse for Concho County, and Oscar Ruffini oversaw the construction, which was completed in 1886. The three-sectioned mansard roof is elaborately decorated with dormers, oval windows, and cornice and trim made of galvanized iron. The rusticated cream-colored limestone walls contrast with the

smooth stone quoins and stringcourse between the floors. The first floor houses the county offices; the second floor is occupied by a large courtroom. The original pressed metal ceilings and wooden stairwells have been preserved.

PRESIDIO COUNTY COURTHOUSE

Marfa. 1886
Alfred Giles. Architect

On July 4, 1910, the citizens of Marfa and Presidio County celebrated Independence Day with a morning parade around the courthouse square. The participants then retired for lunch and rest before returning to the courthouse for an evening dance in the district courtroom. As one young girl described the scene: "The night of the fourth is one of the wildest nights of the year.... A dance is only fitting and the courthouse provided the dance floor ... all you needed were your feet." There were no fireworks, but as the dance ended, intoxicated revelers took to the streets and fired their six shooters into the night.[60]

Marfa is located on the Marfa Plateau of the Chihuahuan Desert of West Texas. By a vote of 392–302, Marfa became the county seat of Presidio County in 1885. The lonely little town was a treeless watering spot for some of the 60,000 head of cattle that roamed the area. Local ranchers and business leaders quickly moved to fund construction of a courthouse. The result was a three-story Second Empire masterpiece, known affectionately as the "Grand Old Lady." It remains one of the most impressive courthouses in Texas.

The octagonal tower, metal-covered cupola and Goddess of Justice are powerful symbols that can be seen for miles.

The corner pavilions are topped with a steep-sloped mansard roof and wrought iron cresting. Three-story, pedimented pavilions mark the entrances. The outer walls were built with red bricks made at a nearby ranch. They were covered with a pale salmon-colored stucco in 1929.

Prior to being commissioned as architect to design a new courthouse for Presidio County, Alfred Giles designed a magnificent courthouse for El Paso County, which also was completed in 1886. His work in El Paso was tainted by accusations of corruption, which damaged Giles' reputation. When bids for the design and construction of the new courthouse were accepted, James H. Britton was awarded the construction contract, but there is no record that an architect was chosen. Giles was never officially named as the architect, but it is clear that he designed the building.[61]

The "Grand Old Lady" is one of the state's most prized courthouses. In 2000, after extensive research and planning, restoration began and the building was rededicated in 2002.

LEON COUNTY COURTHOUSE

Centerville. 1886
William Johnson. Architect

In 1861, an overwhelming number of voters of Leon County ardently supported secession. Soon after war was declared, boys from across the county gathered on the courthouse square in Centerville to enroll in the Confederate Army. They chose a nickname, the Leon County Hunters, and were mustered into Company C of the Fifth Texas Regiment of the famed Hood's Texas Brigade. With great fanfare they marched from the county seat to join General Robert E. Lee's army in Virginia.[62] During four years of war, the boys from Leon County fought in every major engagement, and many of them never returned. At Second Manassas, under the command of Colonel Jerome Bonaparte Robertson, the company led an assault against a New York regiment and took horrendous casualties, the highest the Texas Brigade would suffer in the war. The day after the battle, the survivors buried their friends and neighbors on a Virginia hillside. In 1865, when the young men returned to Leon County, they had earned a more appropriate nickname, the "Bloody Fifth."[63]

The design of this small Renaissance Revival building is more typical of courthouses built during the antebellum period. This is the second courthouse built on the courthouse square.

This modest public building has very little ornamentation. Four Corinthian columns frame the entrance, and two brick string-courses between the first and second floors decorate the exterior.

The Leon County Courthouse is currently in very poor condition. Civic and political leaders in Centerville hope to repair and restore the building, and have received financial assistance from the state and local citizens.

BREWSTER COUNTY COURTHOUSE

Alpine. 1888
Unknown Architect

In November of 1888, Brewster County Judge T.S. Brokenbrow canvassed the votes for county judge and declared his opponent, Wigfalls Van Sickle, the winner by four votes. Within days of the election, Judge Brokenbrow learned that a voting box had been illegally moved eight miles from the G-4 Ranch at Chisos Springs to a line camp ranch house at Agua Frio. All of the votes had been cast for his opponent, and the judge sued to throw out eleven votes and retain his judgeship. Van Sickle entered a counterclaim alleging that on the night before the election, friends of the judge had collected twenty-seven Mexican workers and herded them into the courthouse, kept them there until the polls opened and voted all of them in favor of Brokenbrow. The district court rendered a decision in favor of Van Sickle, and the Texas Supreme Court upheld the decision. The Honorable Wigfalls Van Sickle became the new county judge of Brewster County.[64]

Brewster County is located in the Trans-Pecos region of West Texas. It is the largest county in Texas, encompassing more than 6,000 square miles. When the county was organized in 1887, officials quickly ordered a courthouse to be constructed in the new county seat of Alpine. There are no records as to the architect of the Second Empire building.[65]

The dark red bricks were made in kilns at Ranger Canyon near Alpine. The base of the building is of rusticated limestone with a

brick belt course separating the first and second stories. This simple building has a mansard-like roof made of standing-seam tin with small dormers and stilted arched windows.

WHARTON COUNTY COURTHOUSE

Wharton. 1889
Eugene Thomas Heiner. Architect

In 1888, Wharton County Judge W. J. Croom and his commissioners announced plans to build a new courthouse. Opposition to the proposal was quick and heated, led by a local rancher named Able "Shanghai" Pierce. Wharton was a dangerous place with a bar-room killing almost every Saturday night, and even young girls carried pistols to and from school. With the county close to bloodshed, the governor ordered a company of Rangers to Wharton to keep the peace. Pierce and his lawyers filed an injunction against the judge and Houston architect Eugene T. Heiner, restraining them from demolishing the old courthouse and ordering them to appear before the Federal Court in Galveston to show cause why a permanent injunction should not be issued. Before the writ could be served, the judge and his commissioners cut a hole in the roof of the wooden frame courthouse. When the judge could get half his body through the hole, he threw out his hat and yelled, "Come on boys, let's go!" A peaceful settlement was finally reached between the parties, the old building was demolished and a stylish new courthouse took its place on the county square.[66]

Eugene T. Heiner designed nineteen county courthouses and seventeen jails in Texas. This Second Empire design with its Italianate influences is well-proportioned and typical of the popular styles of the period. The brick exterior walls are trimmed in Austin limestone.

The second-floor district courtroom is two stories tall with a pressed metal ceiling.

In 1900, Wharton was struck by a massive hurricane which greatly damaged the structure. In 1935, county leaders wanted a larger and more contemporary building. The walls were covered with stucco, the tower and roofs were removed and additions were made to the corners. The denatured structure was a disappointment. The restoration of the courthouse is one of the most ambitious in the state, and when completed, this public building will be returned to its original nineteenth-century condition.

HILL COUNTY COURTHOUSE

Hillsboro. 1890
Wesley Clark Dodson. Architect

On the night of January 1, 1993, the Hill County Courthouse erupted in a devastating fire. While Hillsboro residents watched in horror, the 1890 structure was engulfed in flames. The seven story clock tower and the roof collapsed and gutted the once proud building. Firefighters fought the blaze all night, but the building could not be saved. All that remained in the morning were the structure's outer walls.[67]

To the families of Hillsboro, the old courthouse was part of the fabric of their lives. County leaders and citizens were resolute that the courthouse would be rebuilt. It was faithfully restored to its former glory and reopened in 1999.[68]

W.C. Dodson used similar architectural plans and materials for several of his courthouses, but each has its own distinctive features. This grand building is three stories tall, and with the bell and clock tower, stands seven stories. The courthouse is the tallest structure in Hill County and is visible for miles. This elegant building is a Second Empire design with Italianate and Classical Revival influences.

The exterior walls are made of ivory-colored rusticated limestone with banded, dressed limestone columns, and bases, pilasters and trim around the doors, windows and cornice. The entire tower is covered with tin shingles in a diamond pattern.

The three-story portico entrances are large and dominant.  Positioned on a sturdy one-story base, free-standing Corinthian columns support a pediment with a deep arch. They are a dramatic statement of the building's importance to the citizens of Hill County.

THROCKMORTON COUNTY COURTHOUSE

Throckmorton. 1890
Martin, Byrnes and Johnston. Architects/Builders

In 1856, Lieutenant Colonel Robert E. Lee was assigned to command two squadrons of a U.S. Army regiment stationed at Camp Cooper along the Clear Fork of the Brazos River, which was east of the Comanche reserve known as the "Staked Plains." It was the edge of the wilderness, and for nineteen months, Lee would call the lonely camp his "Texas home." There were no buildings; the men lived in tents, exposed to the elements and the Comanches. Much of the country had never been explored or mapped by a white man. His routine consisted of long patrols into the vast wild country searching for roaming Comanches. It was a desolate and dangerous experience for the young officer who four years later would command the largest army of the Confederacy.[69] Little evidence remains of Camp Cooper, which was located some 17 miles south of the city of Throckmorton.

This sturdy Second Empire building was built with native limestone and features a mansard roof. During the late 1880s, the style was a popular one in the mostly isolated counties of West Texas. The firm's design for the Stonewall County courthouse was almost identical, with a large courtroom located on the second floor. Martin, Byrnes and Johnston designed and constructed courthouses and jails for several West Texas counties including Kent, Hamilton, Mitchell and Reeves.

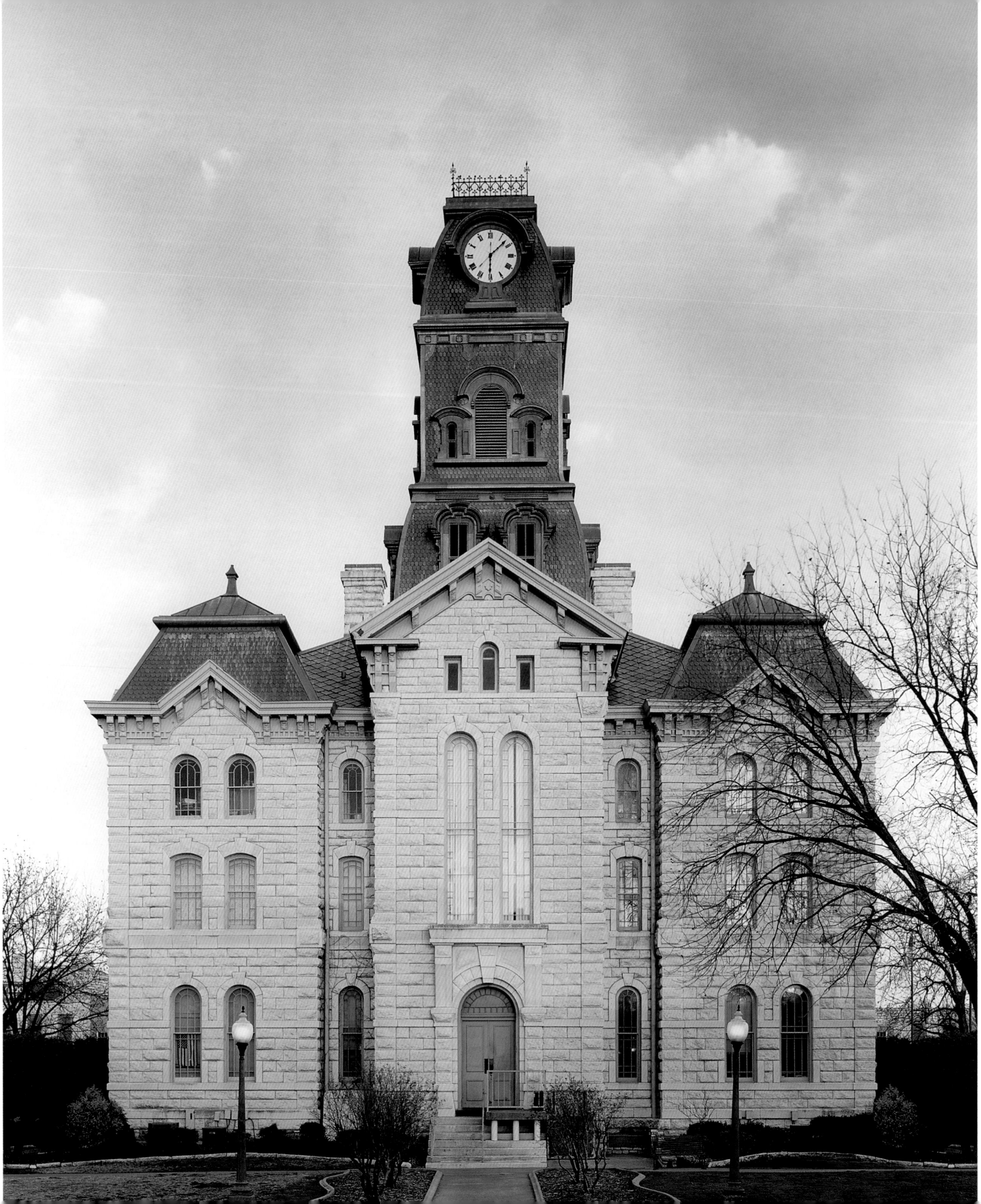

HOOD COUNTY COURTHOUSE

Granbury. 1890

Wesley Clark Dodson. Architect

Hood County was created one year after the end of the Civil War in 1866 by an act of the Eleventh Texas Legislature. The county was named after Confederate General John Bell Hood of Kentucky, who was revered in Texas because of his command of the famed Texas Brigade. The new town and county seat were named for one of his officers, Texas Confederate general Hiram Bronson Granbury, a lawyer and county judge before the war. He was killed in the Battle of Franklin in 1864. Twenty-nine years after his death, Granbury's remains were re-interred in the Granbury Cemetery at a ceremony attended by over 5,000 citizens, including "Men who had followed his impetuous charges, who had seen the magnificent flash of his sword." A statue of the general was erected on the courthouse square, which still stands today.[70]

This exemplary three-story Second Empire courthouse, the third built on the courthouse square, and most of the Victorian commercial buildings surrounding it are made from native limestone blocks quarried nearby. The county seat of Granbury has one of the most faithfully preserved nineteenth century courthouse squares in Texas.

W.C. Dodson employs the basic composition that he utilized for courthouses in Lampasas, Parker and Hill counties with the same successful result. A projecting entrance pavilion,

two recesses on each facade of the structure, mansard roof pavilions and a three-story clock tower rising above a convex mansard roof are hallmarks of Dodson's patented design.

FAYETTE COUNTY COURTHOUSE

La Grange. 1891

James Riely Gordon. Architect

Fayette County was originally part of Stephen F. Austin's first colony in Texas. These early colonists were known as the Old Three Hundred. In 1837, the citizens of the area along the Colorado River petitioned the new Texas Congress to become one of the first counties in the Republic. They named their county after the Marquis de Lafayette, and the county seat of La Grange was named after the French patriot's chateau.

By 1838, Fayette County had become one of the most advanced and populous parts of Texas. When the decision was made during the Second Congress to move the capital farther from the Mexican border, the choice was between two of the republic's most important cities. La Grange lost to Houston by one vote.[71]

This beautiful Romanesque Revival building is the county's fourth courthouse. It is one of the best examples of the popular use of polychromatic features on public buildings during the period. The Muldoon blue and Pecos red sandstone, Burnet granite and Belton white limestone were quarried in Texas. The roof is made of slate and Spanish tile. The clock tower rises 100 feet above the building.

The decorative features of this building are elaborate, such as an American eagle carved on a stone slab above the main entrance and a whimsical gargoyle perched atop a checkerboard-faced pediment.

The courthouse has undergone a complete restoration,  returning the building to its pristine 1891 design. Preservation efforts included restoring a thirty-foot-square central courtyard, which had cast iron sculptures, tropical plants and a fountain, according to Gordon's original design.

Like its twin building in Victoria, the doors to the courtroom were placed around the open space, providing light and ventilation.

The Fayette County Courthouse and its surrounding grounds have undergone a complete restoration, and it was officially rededicated in 2005.

COLORADO COUNTY COURTHOUSE

Columbus. 1891
Eugene Thomas Heiner. Architect

Columbus was one of the first settlements of Stephen F. Austin's colony. In 1836, with Santa Anna's army in close pursuit, Sam Houston's retreating army burned all of the town's buildings. When the county was organized later that year, judicial proceedings were held under a large oak tree on the public square of Columbus. The completion of the county's fourth courthouse on the same site began with a large public celebration in February of 1891. Cheering citizens were entertained by the Weimer Band for the ceremony. After the speeches by county politicians and local leaders, a grand ball was held in the large district courtroom, and dinner was served by the ladies cemetery association in the county courtroom. The old oak tree still stands near the present courthouse.[72]

Designed in Renaissance Revival style in 1890 by Houston architect Eugene T. Heiner, the Colorado County Courthouse originally featured a tall clock tower. In 1909, the tower and most of the roof were destroyed by a tornado. It was replaced by an impressive copper dome, resting on a square drum and positioned directly above the second-story district courtroom.

The district courtroom is imposing with windows that extend from the floor to the ceiling, and dramatic woodwork. The interior glass skylight of the dome was discovered by preservationists when a false ceiling was removed during restoration of the second-floor courtroom.

EDWARDS COUNTY COURTHOUSE

Rocksprings. 1891
Ben Davey and Bruno Schott. Architects

On November 2, 1910, twenty-year-old Antonio Rodriguez was charged with killing Mrs. Lem Henderson on her ranch near Rocksprings. He was arrested by a posse of lawmen the next day and taken to the county jail near the courthouse. Two days later, a mob broke into the jail and dragged the defendant from his cell. Rodriguez was lynched and burned at the stake.[73] When the news of the brutality and swiftness of his execution reached Mexico, his death became an international crisis. Mobs stormed the streets of Mexico City and the border towns along the Rio Grande. The rioters burned American flags and attacked American businesses. Both governments raced to control the violence and

calm relations between the two countries. The Texas press reported extensively on the rioting in Mexico, but gave little coverage to the execution of Rodriguez.[74] The *Houston Daily Post* editorialized that Antonio Rodriguez had, "got nothing more than his due."[75]

This solid Romanesque Revival courthouse is the second for Edwards County and is still an active civic building. Like other substantial structures in Southwest Texas, the native limestone was quarried near the building site. This sturdy and unadorned structure was severely damaged by a fire in 1898, which destroyed most of the county records. In 1927, a deadly tornado killed seventy people in Rocksprings and blew off the roof.[76]

DONLEY COUNTY COURTHOUSE

Clarendon. 1891

C.H. Bulger and Isaac H. Rapp. Architects

In 1878, the Reverend Lewis Henry Carhart, a minister of the Methodist Episcopal Church of the state of New York, had a vision. He and his congregation purchased 343 sections of flat land at the junction of Carol Creek and the Salt Fork of the Red River on the empty plains of the Panhandle. His "Christian Colony" consisted only of families of high breeding and temperance with a strict adherence to the Methodist faith. They sailed from New York City to the Gulf Coast and then traveled the long journey across the state to the town site. He named the new town Clarendon after his wife, Clara, and proclaimed it free of gambling and liquor. Wood was hauled two-hundred miles to build a Christian school, with a goal of one day establishing a college. The cowboys had little patience with the Clarendon Christian Temperance Colony. They quickly dubbed it the "Saint's Roost" and kept their distance. Clarendon was chosen the county seat in 1882, but when the railroad arrived in 1887, the courthouse and the town were moved six miles, and Old Clarendon ceased to exist.[77]

This Romanesque Revival courthouse is one of the oldest active courthouses in the state. The Dallas architectural firm of Bulger & Rapp atypically designed each side of the building. The asymmetrical exterior walls are of St. Louis-pressed bricks and light-colored limestone. The structure sits on a solid base  of quarry-faced ashlar masonry, which may have been taken from an earlier courthouse. The locally quarried stone was not only important structurally, but also for its decorative features, including the lintels for the doors and windows and a wide second-floor stringcourse.

The old building was severely damaged by a tornado in the 1930s. As a result, county leaders remodeled the building, removed the third floor, the upper section of the prominent square corner tower and the conical turret roof. Thanks to the Texas Historic Courthouse Preservation Program, the building has undergone a complete restoration, including the return of the third floor and tower. The interior of the courthouse contains a number of extant furnishings and finishes, including stained glass windows, hardwood floors and original courtroom furniture. Today, the Donley County Courthouse looks much as it did in the early 1890s. It was officially rededicated by county leaders in 2003.

DALLAS COUNTY COURTHOUSE

Dallas. 1891

Maximillian Anton Orlopp. Architect

When the fourth courthouse to occupy the public square was destroyed by fire, Dallas County officials acted quickly. They wanted a public building that would signal the city's economic and cultural importance. Maximillian Anton Orlopp was commissioned to design the new monument. He was born in Brooklyn, New York, in 1859 to German immigrants. He graduated from the United States Naval Academy and served in the U.S. Corps of Engineers before establishing the architectural firm of Orlopp & Kusener in Little Rock, Arkansas.

The massive structure known affectionately as "Old Red" was started in 1890 and completed two years later. It initially had an elaborate 205-foot central clock tower, but it was removed in 1919 when county leaders feared strong North Texas winds would topple it. The tower's 4,500-pound bell and four nine-and-one-half-foot clock faces were demolished and sold for scrap. [78]

This imposing Richardson Romanesque design is a classic example of one of the most popular and sophisticated styles of the era. Pecos red sandstone, Texas red granite and Arkansas blue granite are employed in a mass of contrasting polychromatic patterns. More than three-hundred arched, curved and rectangular windows circle the building. The eight large circular

turrets once were dwarfed by the massive central clock tower. Originally sitting atop "Old Red" were four terra cotta griffins made by a firm in Indianapolis; only two remain on their perch. [79]

In 1938, a county referendum that called for the demolition of the courthouse and the construction of a more contemporary building was defeated. Today, Dallas County preservationists and political leaders are working with the Texas Historical Commission to restore "Old Red" to its former glory. Their plans include renovating the interior of the courthouse and rebuilding the soaring clock tower. When the restoration is complete, "Old Red" will look much as it did in 1892.[80]

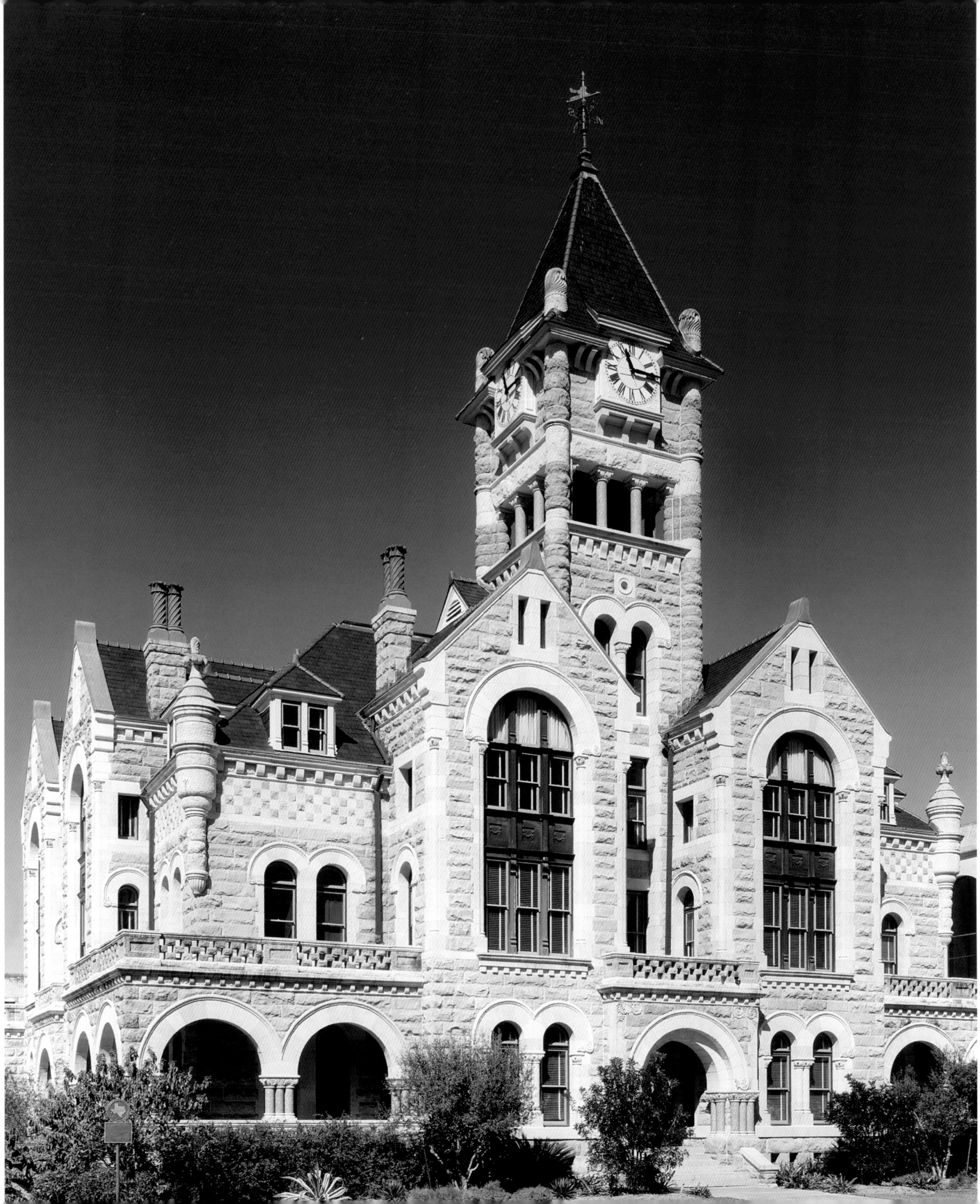

VICTORIA COUNTY COURTHOUSE

Victoria. 1892

James Riely Gordon. Architect

Pompeo Luigi Coppini was born in Italy in 1870. He studied at one of the finest art schools in Florence, and at sixteen, with little money and unable to speak English, the young sculptor immigrated to America. He moved to San Antonio in 1901, and during his 15 years in Texas, he created many of his most important and enduring works. Major monuments on the grounds of the State Capitol and bronze statues at Baylor University and the University of Texas at Austin made him famous. When the Victoria chapter of the United Daughters of the Confederacy planned to erect a statue to honor the county's soldiers, Coppini pleaded with them to allow him to design the memorial, pledging it would be unlike any of the many Confederate statues being erected on courthouse squares across the state. In 1911, his statue of a resolute Confederate soldier was placed on a public square near the courthouse. It is one of his most brilliant works.[81]

The Allegheny County Courthouse in Pittsburgh, Pennsylvania, is considered one of Henry Richardson's finest Romanesque masterpieces, and it was clearly the inspiration for J. Riely Gordon when he designed the Victoria and Fayette county courthouses.[82] Both buildings are close copies of one another and have an almost identical floor plan with a central open courtyard, yet they maintain their own individuality. When Victoria County's cathedral-like building was restored and remodeled in 1998, the thirty-foot open courtyard was eliminated.

This beautiful public building ranks as one of Gordon's most elegant designs. The massive two-story arched windows were created to mark the main courtroom and bring much needed light and ventilation to the interior. The numerous second-floor balconies, arched loggias and entryways were a favorite Romanesque characteristic of Gordon's work.

The rugged limestone and arcades gives this building a monumental sense of governmental power. The use of gray and cream colors for accents such as the artful chimneys and the checkerboard stonework add to the building's character.

ERATH COUNTY COURTHOUSE

Stephenville. 1892
James Riely Gordon. Architect

W hen a decision was made by county leaders to build a new courthouse, J. Riely Gordon was already well-known in the county, having designed two other buildings in Stephenville, including the town's largest bank near the courthouse square. Competing with twenty other architects, he won the commission with a dramatic design. S.A. Tomlinson submitted the successful bid to construct the new towering edifice with a bid of $65,000, which was $10,000 less than the county had budgeted.[83]

This Romanesque Revival courthouse was constructed of white limestone from the Leon River and garnet-colored sandstone that was quarried and shipped from Pecos County. As in his other designs, J. Riely Gordon's superb sense of color and detail are evident in this stately building. The polychromatic structure is three stories high with a solid tripped roof clock tower that rises 95 feet.

Most courthouses of the era emphasized corner and entrance pavilions, but in this composition, Gordon created two protruding intermediate bays topped with triangular pediments, a design he utilized in courthouses for Fayette and Victoria counties.

The interior of the building is finished in East Texas pine and features pink and gray marble tile floors in a checkerboard pattern. The stairways were constructed with cast and wrought iron. The courthouse for Erath County was faithfully restored and rededicated in 2002. It is the county's third courthouse on the square.

MILAM COUNTY COURTHOUSE

Cameron. 1892
Jacob L. Larmour and Arthur Osborn Watson. Architects

O n the night of April 9, 1874, a fire destroyed the three-year-old courthouse. No one knew what caused the blaze. One rumor suggested the building was burned to destroy the evidence of a pending trial. Others were convinced the fire was started to force the county seat to be moved to the railroad town of Rockdale. Before county commissioners would approve the construction of a new building, an election was called to settle the question. Cameron defeated Rockdale by a vote of 1,861 to 1,618. A new courthouse was built, and Cameron remained the county seat.[84]

This beautiful Renaissance Revival structure is the sixth courthouse constructed for Milam County on the original courthouse square. The cream-colored limestone building was designed by Austin architects Jacob L. Larmour and A.O. Watson. Like most interpretations of the period, the courthouse is built on a cruciform plan, with corridors passing through the building on both axes. Most county offices are on the first floor and a large district courtroom is located on the second floor.

The quarry-faced ashlar masonry is complemented by the cut-stone stringcourses. The decorative balconies are not functional. The north and south facades of the building are identical, as are the east and west fronts, with a central tower rising above the mansard roof. The clock tower is covered in sheet metal, and atop the cupola stands a Statue of Justice.

During the 1930s, the building was significantly remodeled, including the removal of the tower and many ornamental details, which changed the character of the building. When the Statue of Justice was taken from her perch, it was discovered that she had been used through the years for target practice. As a participant in the Texas Historic Courthouse Preservation Program, the building was faithfully restored to its former grandeur and was rededicated in 2002.

LLANO COUNTY COURTHOUSE

Llano. 1892
Jacob L. Larmour and Arthur Osborn Watson. Architects

Over 180,000 Texas men and women joined the armed forces during World War I. In 1918, Texas National Guard units were mobilized and assigned to the Rainbow Division under the command of General John J. "Black Jack" Pershing. When the Americans landed in France, the Doughboys from Texas moved quickly to the front and fought side by side in the trenches with their French allies.[85] In one day of heavy fighting during the Meuse-Argonne offensive, 66 officers and 1,227 troops from the Texas Division were killed; it was an inferno. Texas lost almost 6,000 soldiers in World War I,[86] and after the armistice was declared and the veterans returned home, monuments to their sacrifice were erected on many courthouse squares across the state.

This 1892 Romanesque Revival structure replaced a courthouse designed by Alfred Giles that was destroyed by fire in 1886. This is the fourth courthouse for Llano County. The building has three corner pavilions and a uniquely positioned corner tower. Four tall Roman arched windows distinguish the clock tower. The original tower was extensively modified in 1913, and county leaders and preservationists are currently restoring it to its 1892 design.

This bronze monument by a local sculptor honors the heroic young men from Llano County who died in the Great War. It was dedicated on the courthouse square in 1928 by Governor Dan Moody.

SUTTON COUNTY COURTHOUSE

Sonora. 1891

Oscar Ruffini. Architect

In 1887 when the Texas Legislature established Sutton County, life on the western edge of the Edwards Plateau was hardscrabble for the twenty families that crowded around the area's only water hole at Winkler's Well. Water was scarce, and without a steady supply, raising a family or feeding a herd of cattle was almost impossible. They named their small frontier town Wentworth, which boasted a Masonic Lodge that doubled for a school, a windmill and a horse-drawn drill.

Two miles north of Wentworth, another group of determined families established their settlement and called it Sonora. When both communities applied to be designated the county seat, Wentworth had a distinct advantage because of its stable water supply. During the campaign, a well was successfully drilled on the courthouse grounds in Sonora, tipping the election against Wentworth. Within ten years, the town of Wentworth ceased to exist.[87]

This is the only courthouse that Sutton County has ever had. Its Second Empire style was popular on the Edwards Plateau and was used frequently by architects Oscar Ruffini of San Angelo and his brother, F.E. Ruffini of Austin. The rusticated cream-colored limestone exterior walls and smooth stone stringcourses topped by a prominent mansard roof, instead of a tower, were Ruffini trademarks. The exterior of this tastefully designed courthouse was restored and rededicated in 2002.

In spite of the restoration work that has been completed, years of gradual deterioration have caused significant damage to the interior. Extensive repairs are planned to stabilize the old building.

GRIMES COUNTY COURTHOUSE

Anderson. 1894
F.S. Glover. Architect

I n 1934, Bonnie and Clyde were at the height of their rampage of violent crime across Texas. Two members of their gang were captured after an armed robbery in Limestone County, convicted and incarcerated in the State Prison in Huntsville. On two occasions they managed to escape, the second time in a blaze of gunfire. On a foggy January morning, they were working in the fields of a prison farm when Clyde Barrow suddenly appeared in a fast moving car and opened fire with his machine gun. The two convicts found loaded pistols hidden in the underbrush and killed one of the guards while making their escape. The arrest of the gangsters after a statewide manhunt made headlines across Texas. Joe Palmer was Bonnie and Clyde's getaway driver, and when his murder trial commenced in the Grimes County Courthouse, the big courtroom was filled with the law enforcement officers who had been hunting him. The jury quickly found the defendant guilty and sentenced him to death in the electric chair.[88] Four months later, with his appeals denied, Joe Palmer was put to death on "Old Sparkey."[89]

Placed at the highest point of the town's center and with its tall wooden cupola overlooking the countryside, this well-balanced Italianate structure dominates the small town of Anderson, which has remained the county seat since the county

was formed in 1837. This is the county's third courthouse built on this site. A participant in the Texas Historic Courthouse Preservation Program, the building was restored and rededicated by Grimes County in 2002.

The second-floor district courtroom is accessible by exterior as well as interior stairs. During the decades of segregation in Texas, black citizens were required to use a separate, back-door stairwell to enter.

The white limestone-trimmed quoins are used effectively to contrast with the handmade buff-colored bricks. One exterior wall and the foundation of an earlier courthouse destroyed by fire are incorporated into the present structure. This building has survived two fires.

CALDWELL COUNTY COURTHOUSE

Lockhart. 1894
Henry E.M. Guidon. Architect

By 1870, Lockhart was known as "the place where they kill a man every day." Most men carried pistols, and gunfights were a common occurrence around the courthouse square. When two young boys started shooting the chickens on the courthouse grounds, the sheriff called on them to stop, and they shot and killed him.[90] During the 1858 campaign for governor, Sam Houston debated his opponent before the citizens of Lockhart. It was a social event, with the town's leading families in attendance. When the remarks of both men became heated and personal, their supporters drew their guns. Once the gentlemen were restrained and order was restored, lunch was served by the women of the county.[91]

This exemplary Second Empire building is almost identical to the Goliad County Courthouse. The design of both buildings is generally attributed to Alfred Giles, but the original plans were prepared by Henry E.M. Guidon. At the time Guidon submitted his proposal to the county commissioners of Goliad County, he was not with the firm of Alfred Giles. Few architects of the period copyrighted their designs, and through the years, Giles has received credit for a building that was designed by one of his colleagues.[92]

The use of secondary towers, corner pavilions and a lofty central clock tower is a brilliant combination of different design

elements. The tower holds a four-faced Seth Thomas clock and a 900-pound bell. The polychromatic exterior walls are constructed with cream-colored Muldoon limestone and Pecos red sandstone. The multiple string-

courses add contrast to the elegant structure. Pairs of secondary towers guard the front and rear entrances, while the side entrances are adorned with decorative porticoes. Recessed bays flank all four entrances to the building with projecting pavilions at each corner.

The interior of the courthouse has been modified through the years, but the exterior remains largely unchanged. Positioned in the center of the square, it is the county's third courthouse. Like its twin in Goliad County, the Caldwell County Courthouse is a majestic structure.

GOLIAD COUNTY COURTHOUSE

Goliad. 1894

Henry E.M. Guidon, Partner-in-Charge, Alfred Giles & Guidon. Architects

Goliad stood at one of the oldest and most important intersections in South Texas. The Atascosito Road stretched from Central Mexico to Nacogdoches in East Texas, and the only road from the Gulf Coast to San Antonio passed through the town, yet Goliad struggled to survive. By 1855, Mexican teamsters used these arteries to carry their goods on oxcarts to the busy markets of San Antonio. The competition with Anglo cart drivers carrying the same freight at higher rates caused anger and resentment, and racial feelings ran deep. "The Cart War" erupted in violence: oxcarts were burned, goods were stolen and Mexican drivers were killed by ambush. The violence became so brutal and widespread that the Mexican minister in Washington pleaded with the secretary of state to help. Governor Elisha Pease finally took action and sent a company of Texas Rangers to Goliad to escort the Mexican drivers and stop the killings. Trials were held for the murderers of the Mexican teamsters, and their sentence and execution were carried out on the same day under a towering oak tree on the courthouse square. No one knows for sure how many men were hanged from the old oak. The Goliad Hanging Tree still stands.[93]

This beautiful Second Empire courthouse is one of the state's most elegant public buildings. The coursed beige ashlar masonry is highlighted by cut-stone pilasters and garnet-colored string-courses. The domed mansard roofs and imposing clock tower give the structure a formal dignity.

Architect Henry E.M. Guidon joined the firm of Alfred Giles after first designing a courthouse for Caldwell County. He later teamed with Giles, and they sold the same plans to Goliad County. Giles is generally given credit for designing both courthouses, but the architectural plans were the work of Guidon. The two courthouses were completed in 1894.[94]

This is the fourth courthouse built on the county square. In 1942, a hurricane destroyed the clock tower and cupolas. Local civic and political leaders, working with the Texas Historical Commission, returned the structure to its former beauty. In 2003, the new tower and cupolas were dramatically put in place before a crowd of cheering citizens on the square.

GONZALES COUNTY COURTHOUSE

Gonzales. 1894

James Riely Gordon. Architect

John Wesley Hardin was born in 1853, the son of a Methodist minister. He was smart, handsome and to some, a gentleman. He became the most notorious gunfighter in Texas history, killing over thirty men. He lived for a time in Gonzales and during the harsh Reconstruction period, became a small town celebrity. He boasted that he, "never shot a man that didn't deserve it." After killing a deputy sheriff in Comanche, he escaped to Florida, where he was finally apprehended by Texas Rangers, brought back to Texas for trial and sentenced to serve 25 years in prison. During his incarceration, Hardin taught Sunday school, wrote his autobiography, and studied theology and law. In 1894, after serving 16 years in prison, in spite of repeated attempts to escape, Governor Jim Hogg granted Hardin a full pardon. He was promptly admitted to the bar, returned to Gonzales and established a law practice. In 1895, Hardin moved to El Paso and was murdered by a local constable while he was shooting dice. His last words were: "You have four sixes to beat."[95]

The exterior's red pressed brick was imported from St. Louis and contrasts vividly with the white limestone trim. The prominent arches and corner porches are a characteristic of Gordon's work.

J. Riely Gordon perfectly captured the spirit of Romanesque Revival with his use of a unique cruciform plan. The four entrances to this stately structure were placed at the corners, leading to a  single stairwell in the center of the building. Two faces, which were cast in cement, are found above one corner entrance. The clock and bell towers in Gordon's buildings provided light and ventilation.

The large district courtroom, as in most courthouses of the period, is located on the second floor behind the floor-to-ceiling windows. It features a spacious visitors' balcony and a smaller balcony above the judge's bench.

The courthouse sits on one of the original town squares designated by Anglo-American colonists, when Gonzales was founded in 1825.[96] Gonzales County was organized in 1837, becoming one of the first counties formed after Texas became a republic. This courthouse is the fourth for the county. It was restored in 1998.

SOMERVELL COUNTY COURTHOUSE

Glen Rose. 1894

John Cormack. Architect and Builder

In 1875, Somervell County was established from land taken entirely from Hood County. The first courthouse was in a log cabin near an old mill on the Paluxy River and later moved to the new county seat of Glen Rose. During 1876, construction of a permanent courthouse was commenced at the center of the town square.[97] The builder suffered financial ruin and work on the building was stopped until 1882, when the commissioners' court agreed to fund its completion. It stood for twelve years before it was destroyed by fire along with most of the county's records. The present building was completed in 1893 at a cost of $13,500. In 1902, the clocks on the tower were blown away by a devastating tornado that destroyed 36 buildings in the town,[98] but not the rock solid courthouse.

This modest and unadorned courthouse was constructed with white limestone quarried from the nearby bottom lands of the Paluxy River, which empties into the Brazos River.

It is suitably well-proportioned to the charming small town environment of Glen Rose. Somervell County is one of the smallest counties in the state.

HOPKINS COUNTY COURTHOUSE

Sulphur Springs. 1894
James Riely Gordon. Architect

On a February night in 1894, a fire ravaged the center of the small town of Sulfur Springs, destroying the county courthouse, the jail and several businesses bordering the county square. Within six weeks, Hopkins County leaders commissioned J. Riely Gordon to design a new courthouse, and eighteen months later they accepted their impressive new building at a cost of $75,000, a hefty price for the rural East Texas county. In order to save money, county officials declined to purchase a clock for the lofty tower, which soared over one-hundred feet in the air. The citizens had grown accustomed to the clock atop the old courthouse and petitioned the politicians to add one to the new building. The commissioners were unmoved and announced that if their constituents wanted a clock, they would have to pay for it. One commissioner dismissively proclaimed that if people needed to tell time, they should just look up at the sun. The funds were never raised, and the clock tower still stands today without its timepiece.[99]

Designed by J. Riely Gordon, the Hopkins County Courthouse followed the same fundamental cruciform plan he employed in his other public buildings, including multiple towers, turrets and colorful ashlar masonry. Gordon utilized the lofty bell tower for ventilation and as a center stairwell.

The building features open porches on the third floor, surmounting second-story porticoes and Roman arched entrances. Below the balconies are intricate carvings, including carefully crafted faces. Polychromatic mosaic tile hallways lead to the spiral stairway in the tower.

The second-floor district courtroom is a classic Gordon masterpiece with stained glass windows in the judge's chambers and floor-to-ceiling windows in the courtroom. Hidden behind the judge's bench is a winding stairwell leading to the basement, allowing the judge to quickly exit the building.

The use of rusticated stone exteriors, deep contrasting colors and carefully proportioned details were hallmarks of Gordon's design. Red sandstone and pink granite are used for the building's polychromatic exterior walls. The walls and steps are of polished blue granite.

Originally a camping ground for teamsters traveling to Austin along the old Jefferson Road, Hopkins County was one of the first counties created when Texas joined the Union in 1845. This impressive temple of justice is the county's third courthouse. It is placed not on the county square, but facing it. It was restored and rededicated in 2002 as a participant in the Texas Historic Courthouse Preservation Program.

TARRANT COUNTY COURTHOUSE

Fort Worth. 1895

Gunn & Curtiss. Architects

In 1893, Tarrant County leaders were intent on building the biggest and best courthouse in the state, and certainly one more impressive than the new courthouse in neighboring Dallas County. The search and competition to find a suitable architectural firm to design the great building were intense. The county commissioners ultimately awarded the contract to the prominent Kansas City, Missouri, firm of Gunn & Curtiss. The Tarrant County Courthouse is the only courthouse they designed in Texas. The final cost of the building so angered county citizens that every member of the commissioner's court was voted out of office in the next election.

"Gunn and Curtiss' plans for the new courthouse were selected over Sanguinett and Messer by a 3-2 vote. The courthouse will be 230' long and 150' deep with three stories and a basement with four entrances.... All of the architects agree that this has been one of the longest and hardest fought contests of the kind ever had."[100]

The Tarrant County Courthouse is one of the most impressive public buildings in Texas. This four-story Renaissance Revival edifice is built on a high bluff overlooking the Trinity River.

The exterior pink granite walls are from the same quarry as the

State Capitol, which was completed seven years earlier. The tower is made of iron, covered in copper and stands almost two-hundred feet tall. The carved stonework on the hard rusticated granite is outstanding.

The grand building's interior is filled with artful details. Colorfully painted glass domes are located beneath the central tower and the two wings. The library features an elaborate ceiling that overwhelms the rows of law books below.

During the 1950s, local political leaders considered razing the old building because they thought it interrupted the flow of traffic on Main Street. The cupola was painted silver, and in a show of patriotism, county commissioners placed a large neon American flag atop the stately building's clock tower. Today, the majestic building is the centerpiece of a vibrant and bustling downtown, just as it was in the late nineteenth century.

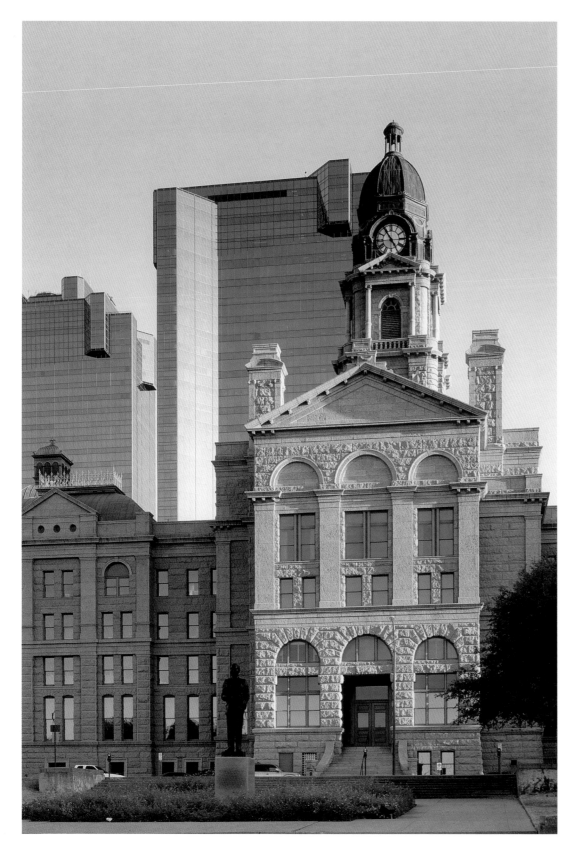

In 1992, with three appellate judges presiding in the large fourth-floor courtroom, attorney George Lott pulled an automatic pistol and opened fire on the lawyers and spectators who filled the room. Two judges and a lawyer were severely wounded; the chief appellate prosecutor was killed, and an attorney was gunned down as he tried to flee down a stairwell. Lott escaped from the building but later surrendered to police.[101] He was found guilty by a Tarrant County jury and executed in 1994 after he refused to appeal his conviction. His rampage was one of the most violent crimes ever committed in a Texas courtroom.[102]

DENTON COUNTY COURTHOUSE

Denton. 1896

Wesley Clark Dodson. Architect

By the spring of 1895, Denton County Commissioners were in full agreement that they needed to replace their crumbling brick courthouse with a new structure, the fifth courthouse for the county. By June, some fifteen architects had submitted proposals. They were all rejected, including the proposal of well-known architect J. Riely Gordon. On the same day, the commissioners gave Gordon two weeks to present a new set of plans. They liked his Richardson Romanesque-styled public buildings, and they admired his design for the Ellis County Courthouse.

When Gordon returned with a new proposal, the politicians studied it for three days before calling for a decision. Two of the commissioners had opposed Gordon as the choice from the beginning, and just before the final vote, one of them claimed in open session that he had been offered a bribe in exchange for his support. It was an embarrassing moment for Gordon, who demanded to know the accuser's name. The dissenting commissioners refused to divulge their source, but the damage was done. Gordon was dismissed and sued Denton County for his fee. He lost in front of a Denton County jury and lost on appeal as well. County commissioners wasted no time in commissioning Waco architect W.C. Dodson to design their courthouse.[103]

This impressive public building dominates the center of Denton as much today as it did more than a century ago. It is an eclectic arrangement of Second Empire, Romanesque Revival and Italianate characteristics. It features a large central octagonal clock tower and four pronounced corner balconies with octagonal towers. The architect utilized a mixture of color and stonework. Most of the limestone came from a nearby quarry, the gray sandstone came from Mineral Wells in Palo Pinto County and eighty-two red granite columns from Burnet County were first polished in Fort Worth before being shipped to Denton.[104]

As part of the renovations in the Texas Historic Courthouse Preservation Program, the exterior masonry and the slate roof on the Denton County Courthouse were reconditioned. Replicas of the original wooden framed windows replaced the worn metal windows. The patterned ceramic tile floors and copper plated hardware were restored to their original luster. In 2004, the Denton County Courthouse was rededicated to commemorate its complete restoration.

The corner balconies distinguish the courthouse from other public buildings of the era. Each of the four entrance pavilions is framed by polished columns and crowned by a pediment and Roman arches.

A Confederate soldier stands guard in front of Denton County's most important building.

ELLIS COUNTY COURTHOUSE

Waxahachie. 1896
James Riely Gordon. Architect

In 1890, Ellis County had become one of the most prosperous counties in Texas. The population in ten years had grown by 50 percent, largely because of the dramatic surge in agricultural production in what many recognized as the wealthiest and most productive part of the state. Agriculture was the strongest economic engine in Texas, and cotton was king. Waxahachie had become the market for more raw cotton than any city in the world. The city had two railway lines, three national banks, four cotton gins, two flouring mills and the most prosperous cotton mills of its day. Waxahachie was booming, and a new courthouse was needed to respond to the county's increased demands and reflect its unbridled success. On July 4, 1895, the cornerstone was leveled with thousands of citizens attending the ceremony and barbecue picnic. The building was completed at an inordinately high cost of $175,000.[105] Ellis County voters were outraged, and in the next election, the county judge and all of the county commissioners were soundly defeated.[106]

This magnificent Richardson Romanesque building is one of J. Riely Gordon's finest works. Built in monumental proportions, with  carefully crafted details and masonry, the Ellis County courthouse is one of the most acclaimed temples of justice in America. It was restored at a cost of $10 million and rededicated in 2002.

Beautifully detailed interior features are found throughout the building, including patterned tiled floors in the hallways and lobbies. Marble wainscoting, iron grillwork, artful plaster, wooden molding, carefully carved woodwork paneling and large oak doors add more beauty. Most of the original furniture was custom-built for the building, and many pieces are still in use.

Quarried from different parts of the state before being transported by rail and wagon to the construction site, gray granite was used for the base of the structure. Burnet County limestone, Pecos red sandstone and rose pink granite were used to create the complex polychromatic exterior walls. German stonemasons were employed to carve the ornamentations, including 21 European-styled stone faces that are surprisingly fanciful. Four large eagles soar above the roof on each side of the building.[107]

The mammoth building stands nine stories tall and encompasses more than 23,000 square feet of floor space. It is supported by a three-foot-thick twisted steel and concrete foundation that supports 12-inch steel beams. The four-sided clock has a wind-up rate of 250 pounds and a striking weight of 800 pounds; it can be heard for miles across the farmlands of Ellis County.[108] The large Roman arched corner entrances and two-story arcaded and colonnaded porticoes allow ventilation into the interior rooms.

LAVACA COUNTY COURTHOUSE

Hallettsville. 1897

Eugene Thomas Heiner. Architect

W hen Lavaca County was organized in 1842, the county seat was located in the small community of Petersburg where court proceedings were held under a live oak tree when the log cabin courthouse burned. In 1852, after two bitter elections to decide the permanent county seat in which fraud was rampant, Petersburg officials claimed victory, destroyed the returns and refused to relinquish the county records. A well-armed committee of over 125 Hallettsville citizens rode to Petersburg, confiscated the documents, loaded them on an ox cart and triumphantly returned to Hallettsville. Petersburg never recovered and soon became a ghost town.[109]

The Lavaca County Courthouse is one of six surviving courthouses of the fourteen designed by Houston architect Eugene T. Heiner. It is the last one the great architect designed. This fine Romanesque Revival building with its tall centrally located tower dominates the town square. It is one of the best examples in the state showcasing the influence of Henry Hobson Richardson.

The picturesque building is noted for its carvings and careful details, such as its arched entryways. The use of Mineral Wells brown sandstone and Mills County gray stone emphasize the building's serious function.

The district courtroom is located on the second floor and is enclosed by floor-to-ceiling arch-framed windows. The windows in the soaring central tower are two stories tall, with a four-faced clock framed in arches. Tall, four-part pyramidal roofs cover the towers.

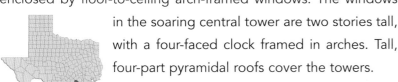

This three-story Richardson Romanesque courthouse is cruciform in design, with a hipped roof and pronounced towers with pyramidal roofs. Below the clock faces, each side of the central tower has narrow windows that are two stories tall. The district courtroom is located on the second floor and is enveloped by floor-to-ceiling arched windows. Arched entryways are featured on all four sides of the building.

WISE COUNTY COURTHOUSE

Decatur. 1896
James Riely Gordon. Architect

"**L**ast Saturday was a gala day at Decatur. The citizens of Wise County assembled at the county capitol to celebrate the laying of the cornerstone of their new courthouse. At an early hour, people in wagons and on horseback began to come in and continued until about 3,000 visitors were present."[110]

This is another fine example of J. Riely Gordon's faithful interpretation of Richardson Romanesque. Gordon repeats his use of turrets, balconies and corner porches leading into a central stairway. The tall imposing clock tower can be seen for miles.

The building features decorative carvings on its ashlar walls composed of two complementary shades of Texas granite. The

interior of this powerful building is as elaborate as its exterior, with extensive use of polished marble furnishings, including the lobbies, stairways and halls. The floors are made of marble tile in a checkerboard pattern.

DeWITT COUNTY COURTHOUSE

Cuero. 1897

Arthur Osborn Watson and Eugene Thomas Heiner. Architects

In 1846, DeWitt County was founded, and its county seat was established in Daniel Boone Friar's home at the intersection of the La Bahia Road and the Victoria-Gonzales Road. Within the next four years, the county seat and courthouse were moved at least four times before the old Spanish town of Cuero was finally chosen. After each close election, there was a recount, an appeal or a decision of the Texas Supreme Court to resolve the contest.[111]

Constructed in the same year, the courthouses in DeWitt and  Lavaca counties were greatly influenced by Henry Hobson Richardson's Allegheny courthouse in Pittsburgh, Pennsylvania, one of the country's most important late nineteenth century buildings.

When the county's two-story wooden courthouse was destroyed by fire in 1894, popular architects A.O. Watson and Eugene Heiner partnered to design this highly polychromatic edifice, utilizing three colors of rusticated sandstone.

This building is characterized by a triple-arcaded, one-story porch beneath the impressive six-story clock tower. The main tower and the corner pavilions have pyramidal roofs of red slate.

The building and grounds are undergoing a major preservation effort as a participant in the Texas Historic Courthouse Preservation Program. Under the guidance of the Texas Historical Commission, the exterior will be restored with the installation of new doors that match the originals and repair of the surviving wooden windows. The Spanish tile roof will be replaced, and the original slate roof will be replicated. The interior, significantly modernized in 1956, will be rehabilitated.

BEXAR COUNTY COURTHOUSE

San Antonio. 1897

James Riely Gordon. Architect

Anderson Hutchinson was one of the first great lawyers and acclaimed jurists in Texas. Trained in Virginia, he practiced law in Tennessee, Mississippi and Alabama before opening a law office in Austin in 1840. Hutchinson was successful and gained notoriety as a brilliant lawyer of great integrity. President Sam Houston recognized his talent and appointed him to serve as the judge of the Western District of Texas. In 1842, Judge Hutchinson was holding court in the Bexar County Courthouse when Mexican forces captured San Antonio, stormed into his courtroom and captured him along with the parties to the lawsuit, the attorneys and the court clerks. They were summarily marched in chains to a Mexican prison. The prisoners endured seven months of incarceration and hardship before their release was negotiated. Judge Hutchinson refused to return to Texas, resigned his judgeship and moved to Mississippi.[112]

In 1891, Bexar County officials advertised nationally for architects to design a new courthouse. First- and second-place prizes of $1,000 and $500, and the opportunity to design a civic building for one of the prominent cities of Texas, drew twenty-seven entrants from across the country. Local leaders unanimously chose the young hometown architect, J. Riely Gordon.[113]

This Romanesque Revival building is the fourth courthouse for Bexar County. It replaced a courthouse designed by Alfred Giles.

The Bexar County temple of justice is the largest historic courthouse in Texas. The exterior stonework was restored and rededicated in 2003 as part of the Texas Historic Courthouse Preservation Program.

The building is a stone giant filling an entire city block, and has been remodeled several times with new additions and interior changes. Only the front three exterior sides of the structure are original. The exterior walls, made of Pecos red sandstone and pink granite, include the careful stonework and monumental proportions that made J. Riely Gordon famous.

The front wall of the mammoth structure features two prominent corner towers. One is topped with a pyramid of green tile, and the other is covered in red tile in a tall one-of-a-kind beehive shape.

Because of the many alterations over time to the building's interior, only the exterior of the historic courthouse retains its nineteenth century integrity. During the late 1920s, the interior was substantially remodeled, and many of the courtrooms from that renovation are extant. Preservationists plan to restore the interior to its 1927 appearance.

CORYELL COUNTY COURTHOUSE

Gatesville. 1897
Wesley Clark Dodson. Architect

I n 1897, local politicians, community leaders and the citizens of Coryell County gathered on Gatesville's public square for a ceremony to level the cornerstone for a new courthouse. After a musical introduction by Mrs. Shadden's orchestra and the appropriate orations by county officials, a blue-gray granite stone weighing 1,825 pounds was lowered into place. Local Masonic leaders deposited souvenirs into a copper box and placed it in the hollowed cornerstone. Included was a photograph of the old courthouse, copies of the county's two newspapers, a vial of salt, a book of formulas, a rock from Lebanon, a box of pills, two boxes of medicine, a bottle of whiskey and a Bible.[114]

The Coryell County Commissioners Court approved plans for a new courthouse and commissioned noted Waco architect W.C. Dodson to design the building for a contracted fee of three and one-half percent of the total building costs. This elegant edifice combines Victorian styles, still highly popular in Texas, with Romanesque Revival features such as the rusticated exterior walls. The cupola holds a Seth Thomas clock and a bell weighing more than 800 pounds. The roof and dome of the cupola are made of metal and copper and topped by a bronze eagle. Cream-colored limestone with contrasting red sandstone trim was used for the exterior walls. Four statues of Liberty and Justice are placed at the north and south entrances. The building was completed in

accordance with highly detailed instructions of the county commissioners.[115]

The central rotunda is octagonal in shape and is formed by the intersection of four entry halls. It rises to a stained glass dome, with the lantern and major dome above. The large second-floor district courtroom and the county courtroom are designed in a uniquely oval shape. The third floor of the building holds the district courtroom balcony and a room for jury deliberations.

Many courthouses of the era were designed with four equally prominent entrances. This courthouse has one main dramatic entrance, and the opposite side of the edifice is clearly secondary in importance. The two entrances at the ends of the structure are identical and modest in design.

Today, this grand temple of justice dominates the town center of Gatesville very much as it did in 1897.

LEE COUNTY COURTHOUSE

Giddings. 1897

James Riely Gordon. Architect

In 1873, citizens of northeastern Bastrop and Fayette counties and the western regions of Burleson and Washington counties petitioned the Legislature to form a new county named after Robert E. Lee. Loyalty to the Confederacy and its heroes, especially among the men who had fought in the war, was still strong eight years after the surrender. As new counties across Texas were created, more than two dozen of them would be named for veterans who had served the Confederacy.[116]

The style of this Romanesque Revival courthouse was based on the cruciform plan used repeatedly by J. Riely Gordon. The corner entrance porches utilize blue granite columns and carved limestone capitals and open into a central hall under the rising, square clock tower. Gordon's design for Lee County is modest and not as embellished as his other courthouses. This is the county's second courthouse. The first was built in 1878 and was gutted by fire, because the firefighters' ladders were too short to reach the upper floors of the burning building.[117]

The rusticated white sandstone arches and wide stringcourses add striking contrasts to the bright red brick walls. The entrances and second-floor balconies are placed at the reentrants of the arms of the cross. The building's roof was originally made of slate and tin.

Lee County is participating in the Texas Historic Courthouse Preservation Program. The exterior walls of this stately courthouse have been restored, and the structure was rededicated in 2004.

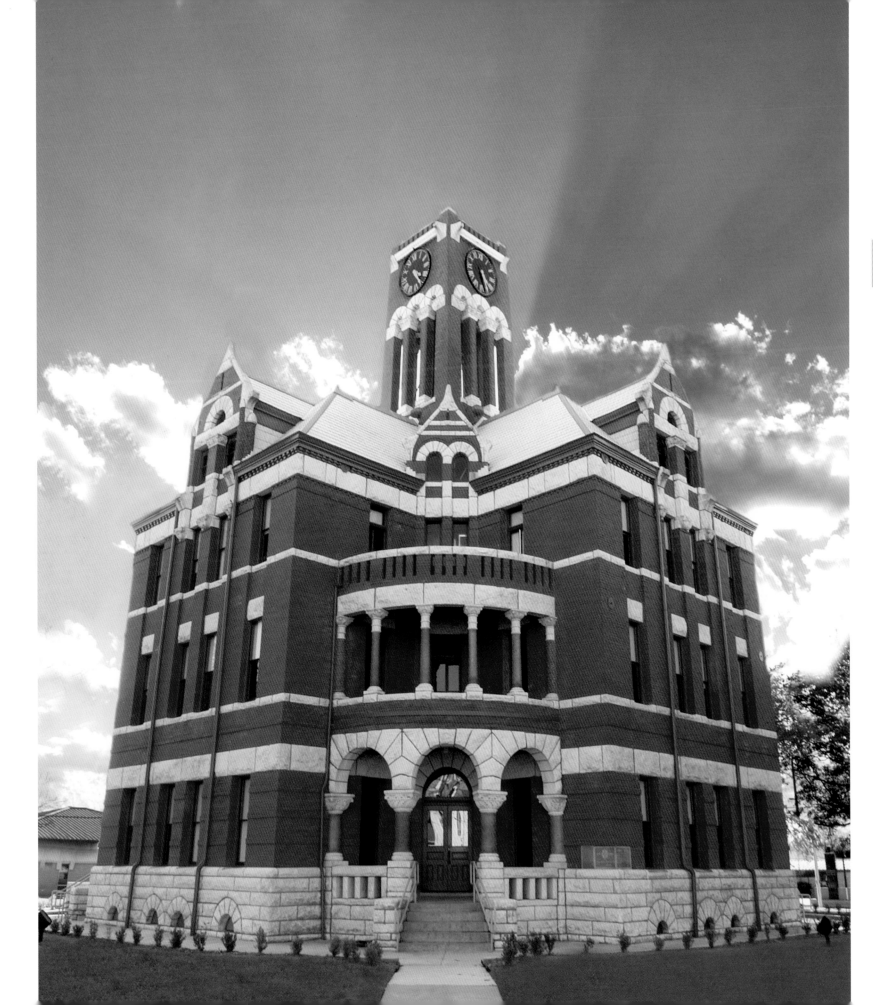

COMAL COUNTY

COMAL COUNTY COURTHOUSE

New Braunfels. 1898
James Riely Gordon. Architect

In 1842, a group of wealthy German noblemen pledged to buy land in Texas and establish settlements for German and other European immigrants. Prince Carl of Solms-Braunfels was appointed Commissioner General of the Society for the Protection of German Immigrants to Texas and purchased land grants primarily between the Colorado and the Llano rivers. One of the sites he chose for a way station was located on the banks of the Comal River. The prince named his new town after his ancestral home of Braunfels, Germany. By 1847, sixty ships had brought more than 7,000 settlers on a two- to three-month voyage across the Atlantic. The new arrivals traveled some 200 miles inland to their new homes. The Society eventually went bankrupt, but the immigrants stayed—enduring disease, Comanche raids and isolation. Many of their descendants still live in the Texas Hill Country.[118]

This second courthouse for Comal County, dedicated in 1899, was designed by J. Riely Gordon in his signature style. The Richardson Romanesque structure was built with locally quarried rusticated limestone in a light gold color. The entrance porches are ornamented by polished pink granite columns supporting the

corner balconies. Like other Gordon courthouses, the corner entrances lead to a central stairway and a massive bell tower. Additions in 1930 and 1966 have enlarged and altered Gordon's original design.

McCULLOCH COUNTY COURTHOUSE

Brady. 1899
William Martin and Peter Moodie. Contractors

When this sturdy courthouse was unanimously accepted by county officials in 1900, it dominated the small town of Brady and the surrounding countryside. It was the largest structure in the county, and for the 1,500 people who lived in McCulloch County, it became their "town hall." Wooden benches stood against the walls of the wide hallways, and they were always filled with people. With the doors and windows open, a breeze kept the building cool, even in the hot Central Texas summers. Church services, lectures, piano recitals,  weddings and holiday celebrations were all held in the courthouse. The third floor contained the county library. The courthouse was "the place for all business and social activities."[119]

A model of Henry Hobson Richardson's Romanesque style, this grand structure is solid and powerful in its simplicity. The rusticated sandstone exterior walls and arched entrance are well-proportioned, as is the dominant clock tower.[120] Although a space is clearly designated on all four sides of the square tower for a clock, one was never installed. In the contract for the courthouse, the county commissioners also required a well, a fifty-foot windmill and water tank.[121]

Twin turrets flank an arched entrance with a dormer positioned above. Projecting pavilions frame two entrances surmounted by simple triangular pediments. The diamond-faced cut stone above the doors is one of the building's few ornamental features.

The owners of the contracting firm of Martin and Moodie in Comanche were not professional architects. They designed and constructed courthouses in Irion and Newton counties.

IRION COUNTY COURTHOUSE

Sherwood. 1901
William Martin and Peter Moodie. Contractors

In 1889, the Texas Legislature carved sparsely populated Irion County from western Tom Green County. Local leaders quickly chose the cowtown of Sherwood as their new county seat. In 1910, the Kansas City, Mexico and Orient Railroad bypassed Sherwood by a few miles and a new railroad town, Mertzon, was built. The struggle to move the county seat was placed on the ballot in 1927, and county voters chose Mertzon over Sherwood by a margin of 286–231. Pursuant to the Texas Constitution, a two-thirds majority was necessary to change the location of county governments, and Sherwood remained the county seat until 1936 when Mertzon won by a vote of 453–222.[122]

Built in 1901, this Second Empire courthouse has long been abandoned in the ghost town of Sherwood, the former county seat of Irion County. Made of quarry-faced ashlar limestone walls, the lonely building has four Roman arched entrances decorated with carved owls. When it was completed, it was the only stone building in the county.

The four facades of the square building are similar with shallow entrance porches. On two sides, the second floor projections are almost even with the building, allowing for two second-floor balconies.

The roof is covered with standing-seam metal, and galvanized iron covers the Classical tower. The bell tower features a false clock, which county legend claims was perpetually set at the time of Abraham Lincoln's death.[123]

CROCKETT COUNTY

CROCKETT COUNTY COURTHOUSE

Ozona. 1902

Oscar Ruffini. Architect

In 1891, the Legislature carved a new county out of the western edge of the Edwards Plateau of southwest Texas. Fewer than two-hundred ranchers and settlers lived near the scarce water holes on the dry plains of southwest Texas. An election was held to choose the county seat between Emerald, the only town in the new county, or the site of a water well seven miles west. When the election returns were canvassed, the watering hole called Ozona became the county seat. The first commissioners' court was convened in a tent stretched under a large oak tree, which still stands near the present courthouse.[124]

This Second Empire edifice features a large convex-curved mansard roof and strong corner pavilions with pyramidal roofs. The ashlar exterior walls are of hand-sawed rusticated limestone blocks. The square building has four identical five-bay facades. A one-story gallery with an iron balcony is placed between the two end pavilions. The distinct string-courses below the second-story arched windows divide the floors.

At the turn of the century, when their courthouse was completed, 1,500 citizens lived in a county of more than 2,800 square miles. The building was the most significant structure in the county. The large second-floor courtroom was used not only for judicial proceedings, it also served as a community center, dance hall and meeting place.

Architect Oscar Ruffini replicated this basic design in a series of courthouses with more proportioned results. Before Ruffini's courthouse in Ozona was completed, its design was out of fashion in the more cosmopolitan centers of the state. This is the second courthouse for Crockett County.

A NEW CENTURY

In 1922, Nathan Lee shot a local Angleton farmer in the back of the neck and killed him. The deceased was found near his home a few days later. *The Angleton Times* headlined the story that "Nathan Lee, Negro" had killed a "white farmer." The local lodge of the Ku Klux Klan sent flowers to the funeral service. In accordance with the Texas Criminal Code, a Brazoria County jury wasted no time in convicting and sentencing Nathan Lee to death by hanging on the courthouse square. One year later, after the defendant's appeals were exhausted, the presiding judge, following the criminal statutes of the state, scheduled the execution on a Friday, thirty days from the date of sentencing, between the hours of eleven o'clock in the morning and sundown. A wooden scaffold was constructed in front of the courthouse, and plans were made for a big crowd of spectators in Angleton with the approach of Black Friday.

The sheriff and his deputies with the appropriate decorum carried out the execution. The condemned man made a short speech from the gallows admitting his guilt and wishing his mother, wife and five children goodbye. After his confession, a hymn was sung at his request, shortly before the trap door was sprung. Nathan Lee died almost instantly from a broken neck and was pronounced dead by two doctors. By order of the court, the body of the deceased was allowed to hang for 15 minutes before being transported to his home. The county sold the scaffold to the highest bidder thirty days later. The execution of Nathan Lee was the last legal hanging in Texas.[125]

The twentieth century dawned on a vibrant and rapidly changing Texas. During the first two decades, Texas experienced phenomenal economic growth that was more diverse and robust than in any previous era. Advances in transportation, primarily because of the expansion of the railroad and an emerging automobile industry, increased communication and intensified the state's modernization. New counties were created as the far corners of Texas were dotted with towns and people. In 1907, on the courthouse square in Marfa, barbecue was served and speeches were made by local dignitaries when electricity came to Presidio County, and by 1910, there were more than one-hundred automobiles in town.[126] The state was maturing in ways no one could have imagined a few years before.

In 1899, the Texas Legislature passed an act requiring that construction of any new public building be submitted to a county's voters for approval before bonds could be issued.[127] This law had a significant influence on the decisions of local leaders; henceforth, county voters had the last say about financing new courthouses. In most instances, it did not slow the funding for new public buildings or the desires of county voters to build larger and more inspiring temples of justice. Competition between counties for prestige and recognition continued just as in previous years.

The new century also brought different tastes, a more enlightened sophistication and an appreciation of new architectural styles for governmental buildings. National trends in architecture were more quickly recognized and adopted by local leaders. Several well-publicized fairs across the country, such as the World's Columbian Exposition of 1893 in Chicago, exhibited new modes of design and had a significant influence on popular tastes across the nation. American architecture was changing, and talented young designers were responding to these national trends by creating new and different concepts for governmental buildings.

Many remote regions of the state remained isolated from these changes, and public architecture reflected this isolationism.

Although the Irion County Courthouse in Sherwood and the Crockett County Courthouse in Ozona were constructed after the turn of the century, their designs were deeply rooted in the nineteenth century and out of fashion before they were completed. In the more developed areas of Texas, change occurred rapidly. County leaders were quick to discard dated norms of design for new concepts and status. The dominant influence of Richardson Romanesque, acclaimed in the 1890s, began to fade in popularity as different classical designs gained favor. The Second Empire and Victorian classical forms that dominated public buildings of the late nineteenth century began to evolve into different modes of design. By the turn of the century, Beaux Arts, Classical Revival and Renaissance Revival ascended as popular concepts for governmental buildings. In addition, technological advances in construction and the availability of a wider source of building materials afforded architects greater flexibility in design and composition.

A new generation of nationally recognized architectural leaders began to have a profound impact on American design, just as Henry Hobson Richardson had in the past century. Louis Sullivan and Frank Lloyd Wright's Prairie School would leave their imprint on public buildings in Texas. Renowned architect Atlee B. Ayres hired the former head draftsman for Frank Lloyd Wright, George Willis,[128] and utilized various degrees of Prairie School ornamentation in his courthouses for Jim Wells, Cameron, Refugio and Kleberg counties.[129] The firm of Lang and Witchell employed one of Frank Lloyd Wright's young apprentices, Charles Barglebaugh.[130] The firm's designs for the interiors of the Johnson and Cooke county courthouses are impressively influenced by Sullivan and Wright.[131]

The two most accomplished Texas architects of the late nineteenth century, J. Riely Gordon and Alfred Giles, continued to prosper during the early years of the twentieth century, primarily because they recognized the emerging national trends and adopted new approaches to design. Two of Gordon's most impressive courthouses were the last he designed in the state. His courthouses for Harrison and McLennan counties, built in 1900 and 1902 respectively, featured impressive domes rather than the imposing towers he had utilized in his earlier designs. Gordon moved to New York in 1902 and left the stage to the new generation of architects.

Unlike most of their predecessors, many Texas architects of the early twentieth century were formally trained and their backgrounds were diverse and structured. Ayres studied at the Metropolitan Museum of Art in New York and practiced in Mexico before establishing his San Antonio firm in 1898. His son, Robert M. Ayres, received his education at the University of Pennsylvania before joining his father in 1924. The impressive breadth of their architectural projects and their progressive designs left an enduring legacy in San Antonio and South Texas. Like Alfred Giles in the previous generation, Ayres became a social and civic leader in San Antonio. In 1915, he was appointed as the first State Architect of Texas and was a statewide leader in upgrading the standards of his profession.[132]

Charles H. Page formed a partnership with his brother, Louis, and their prominent firm of Page Brother (later Page Brothers) would span more than 50 years and leave an indelible mark on Austin. In a remarkable career, Charles Page designed his first courthouse for Hays County in 1908, and the last courthouse designed by the firm he founded was in 1937 for Orange County.

Otto Lang and Frank Witchell, who had worked under the tutelage of J. Riely Gordon, established their firm in Dallas and would collaborate on five courthouses in the state. Talented James E. Flanders of Dallas would design courthouses for Shackelford and Navarro counties. Six courthouses were designed by West Texas architect David L. Castle, and 11 courthouses remain active today that were designed by Henry T. Phelps of Houston.

In the new century, the county courthouse continued to be the preeminent symbol of local rule and the dominant structure of community life, as public officials worked to fund the construction of new governmental buildings in every region of the state. The highly popular classical designs of the day were well suited for a maturing state, and a fresh group of skilled Texas architects was prepared to respond.

HARRISON COUNTY COURTHOUSE

Marshall. 1900

James Riely Gordon and C.G. Lancaster. Architects

In 1839, corruption and lawlessness were rampant in the Redlands of East Texas. Disputes over land titles and fraudulent land claims were part of a larger fight between rival factions to gain control of the land that would become Harrison and Shelby counties. The bitter feud turned to violence, and hundreds of local citizens, judges and lawmen took sides in the bloody conflict that was known as the Regulator-Moderator War. The Regulators gained the upper hand and planned to extend their influence across the new republic. In the summer of 1844, the violence and murder became so rampant that a frustrated President Sam Houston ordered the militia to intervene. With Houston's approval, a peace treaty was negotiated and signed by the leaders of both counties, finally putting an end to the bloodshed.[133]

In this magnificent courthouse, J. Riely Gordon continues the use of his characteristic cruciform floor plan, but his design for Harrison County's temple of justice has clearly evolved. A highly decorated rotunda is lighted through colored glass rather than a clock tower. The pedimented porticoes and dramatic dome are a striking departure from his earlier works. The rusticated pink granite base, marble and buff-colored brick walls are beautifully accomplished. This ornamented structure features soaring eagles with six-foot wingspans that decorate the dome, and a Statue of Justice standing watch from the top of the lantern.

Gordon collaborated with C.G. Lancaster to design this courthouse, continuing use of his cruciform floor plan. The dome is positioned upon a drum and has a decorated sunken paneled ceiling. The impressive cast iron central stair, geometric floor tiles and light fixtures are all original.

First-floor entrances and windows are framed by Roman arches. The upper and lower floors are divided by a cut-stone stringcourse. The windows on the second floor, which includes a two-story courtroom, are spanned with stone lintels. The exterior walls of the upper stories feature two-story pilasters with capitals made of terra cotta and Ionic bases.

This monumental building, the fourth of five courthouses for Harrison County, evokes a state capitol rather than a county seat of government. In 1926, an addition was added to the main structure. The building, which now serves as a museum, and square are currently undergoing restoration to its 1926 condition with partial funding from the Texas Historic Courthouse Preservation Program.

MCLENNAN COUNTY

MCLENNAN COUNTY COURTHOUSE

Waco. 1902
James Riely Gordon. Architect

O n May 8, 1916, a seventeen-year-old black farm hand named Jesse Washington was arrested in Waco for the brutal rape and murder of a fifty-three-year-old white woman. The accused quickly confessed to the crime, and his trial was held seven days later in the McLennan County Courthouse. Passions ran high and the large district courtroom of Judge Richard Munroe was overflowing with angry citizens as the lurid testimony was presented. The trial lasted a little over an hour, and the jury deliberated only four minutes before the defendant was found guilty and sentenced to death. As Washington was about to be removed from the courtroom, the crowd overpowered the bailiffs and dragged him down the back stairs to a waiting mob. A crowd estimated at 15,000 people joined the uncontrolled violence, while the mayor and the chief of police watched from a window in the mayor's office. The mob placed a chain around the guilty man's neck, dragged him through town, hanged him from a tree and then set him on fire. It was hours later when the sheriff retrieved the charred body. Lynching was against the law in Texas, but no one was ever prosecuted for the violent crime, which became known across the nation as "The Waco Horror."[134]

This majestic building with its elaborately decorated dome was a departure from some of J. Riely Gordon's earlier Richardson Romanesque designs. It is similar to the Harrison County  Courthouse and the Arizona State Capitol, which also were designed by Gordon. Waco architect W.C. Dodson supervised the construction. The Beaux Arts Classical building has a sturdy base of rusticated pink granite and smooth white limestone walls. A festooned pediment adorned by an eagle and statues of Justice and Liberty frame the entrance.

Twelve eagles surround the inspiring dome, and a Statue of Justice adorns the lantern. The interior is equally elegant and features a lighted stained glass, domed ceiling.

Appropriately placed on the high ground overlooking Waco, the structure has the look and feel of a state or national capitol.

NAVARRO COUNTY COURTHOUSE

Corsicana. 1905
James Edward Flanders. Architect

On a cold February day in 1848, five county commissioners stood on the high point of a hill overlooking their town. Braced against the winter chill, one by one they took a hammer and drove a wooden stake into the frozen ground. It was not much of a ceremony, but to these pioneers, it was an important moment. This would be the site for the new courthouse at the center of the hundred acres square.[135]

The Navarro County courthouse is a majestic Beaux Arts building designed by J.E. Flanders in 1905. The powerful structure uses Prairie School features on the building's interior.[136] This temple of justice is the fifth courthouse located on the hilltop square. The first courthouse was a log cabin built in 1848, which still stands nearby. The present building replaced a Second Empire style building by F.E. Ruffini, which was declared unsafe by county leaders and destroyed.

The exterior walls are made of red Burnet granite and gray brick. The open tower was originally designed as a bell tower, and a four-sided clock was added in 1923. The square tower is covered in copper and rises three stories above the rotunda and staircases. There has been little change to the exterior of the building.

Behind the bronze statue of the county's namesake, Jose Antonio Navarro, a granite stair entrance leads to Ionic columns

and two pilasters beneath a large pediment. The end pavilions also feature Ionic columns and rounded windows on the top floor.

An elaborate stained glass dome illuminates the interior of the tower, and

decorative Ionic concrete columns are placed throughout. Centered on the second floor, a Lone Star of Texas design can be seen from the higher floor rotunda areas. Marble ornamentation, wood paneling and terrazzo floors are featured in the building's public spaces.

Erected in 1917 as a memorial to the members of the Corsicana Fire Department, a firefighter stands ready on the courthouse grounds.

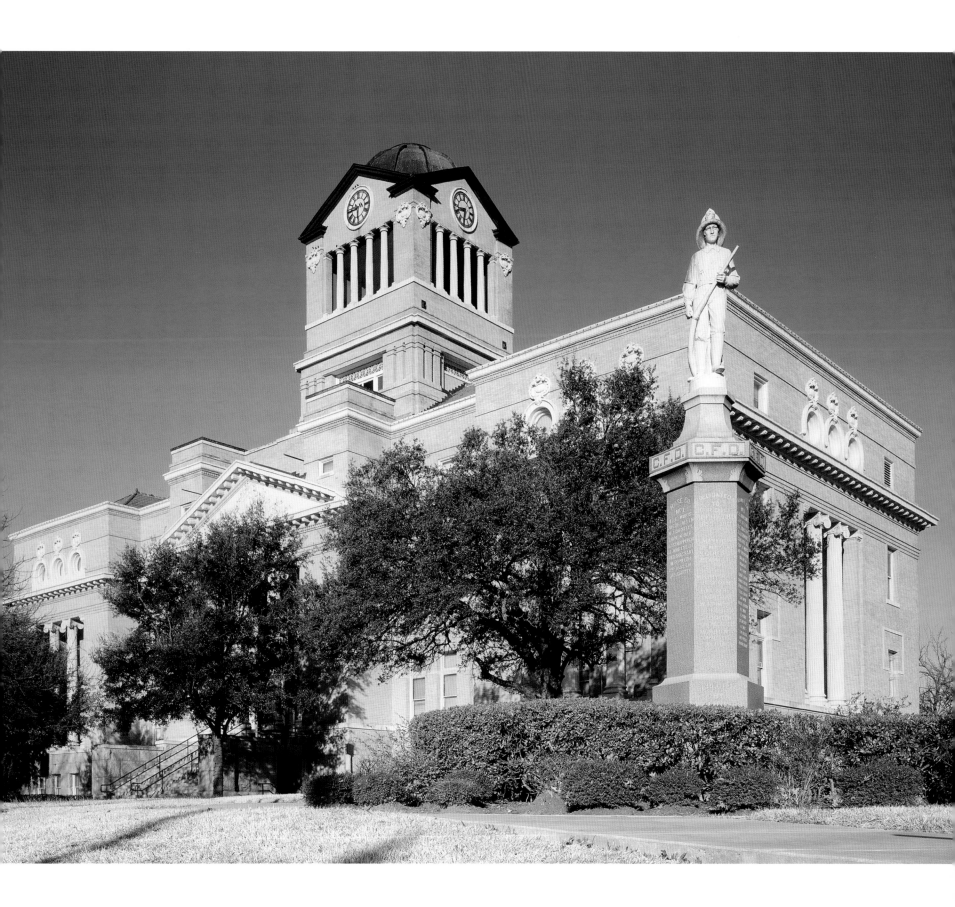

HARTLEY COUNTY COURTHOUSE

Channing. 1906
Otho Gibson Roquemore. Architect

In 1879, the Texas Legislature appropriated three million acres of land in the Panhandle to finance a new State Capitol. A devastating fire had destroyed the old Capitol building, and state officials were intent on quickly building a replacement. A Chicago syndicate of businessmen purchased the land and formed the XIT Ranch in 1882 on a vast unsettled rangeland that covered ten counties. Within a few years, the XIT herds would average over 150,000 head of cattle with over 6,000 miles of barbed wire fence. The XIT dominated life on the high plains. The ranch headquarters was established in the small rail town of Channing in the northwestern part of the Panhandle.[137] When the town was declared the county seat in 1903 after a bitter election, the wooden frame courthouse was loaded on a wagon and moved from Hartley to Channing by XIT cowboys and armed lawmen. The building was later turned into a hotel, when the present courthouse was built in 1906.[138]

Built near the tracks of the Fort Worth and Denver Railroad, this Beaux Arts structure has served Hartley County since 1906. With the exception of a rear addition that was added in 1935, the modest courthouse remains largely unchanged. The front facade of this two story red brick building features four Ionic columns supporting a Palladian entryway. Native sandstone was used for the base and the belt course that encircles the building.

The second floor contains a single courtroom and the judicial chambers, which retain most of their original features, including pressed tin ceilings and ceiling fans.

The courthouse and the adjacent county jail are two of the best preserved governmental complexes in the Panhandle region. Both buildings were initially served by their own water well and lighting system. In an area of the state with few trees, large Chinese elms are planted in a checkerboard pattern on the grounds of the square.

FORT BEND COUNTY COURTHOUSE

Richmond. 1908

Charles Henry Page and Brother. Architects

Almost as soon as he arrived in Texas, wealthy and scholarly Mirabeau Buonaparte Lamar enlisted in Sam Houston's army, insisting on the rank of private. He was a natural leader, and at the Battle of San Jacinto his bravery was unsurpassed. Lamar would become a vice president and president of the Republic of Texas, a veteran of the War with Mexico, a member of the Texas Legislature, the American minister to Nicaragua and Costa Rica, a celebrated poet and one of Fort Bend County's most famous citizens.[139]

This fine Beaux Arts edifice was the first courthouse designed by the firm of C.H. Page and the fourth built in Fort Bend County. It is the nucleus of the original town center of Richmond. It features a copper Statue of Justice standing watch atop a clock on a copper-clad domed roof. This excellent example of Classical Revival features a three-story projecting portico with stone columns and carefully crafted stone capitals. The building has bold corner pavilions topped by copper-covered turrets.

A three-story open rotunda dominates the public space in the building's interior.

The design of the building is based on a basic cruciform plan. The arched windows on the first floor complement the dramatic entrance and are divided from the rectangular windows of the

upper floors. A stone band that encircles the original building contrasts with the beige brick. Significant additions were added to the original structure in 1935 and 1957. The courthouse was restored in 1980.

With a law book and quill in hand, Mirabeau Buonaparte Lamar stands before the temple of justice.

HAYS COUNTY COURTHOUSE

San Marcos. 1908

Charles Henry Page and Brother. Architects

"I will never again fight Jack Hays, who has a shot for every finger on his hand."—Comanche war chief[140]

"Me and Red Wing not afraid to go to Hell together. Captain Jack heap brave; not afraid to go to Hell by himself."—Flacco of the Lipans

"The Indians ... fought under great disadvantage but continued to struggle to the last, keeping up their war songs until all were hushed in death."—Texas Ranger Captain Jack Hays

"You may depend on the gallant Hays and his companions...." —President Sam Houston[141]

Hays County was formed in 1848 and named for Texas Ranger and Indian fighter John (Jack) Coffee Hays, with the support of his former comrades. This is the fourth courthouse for Hays County, and all have been placed on the same site. The former courthouse, designed by F.E. Ruffini, was razed by county officials after the third floor was gutted by fire in 1908.

The Page brothers replicated their design for the Fort Bend County Courthouse in Hays County. The two Beaux Arts buildings, constructed in the same year, are almost identical, including the grand portico with a colonnade of four Corinthian columns. The Statue of Justice does not stand above a four-sided clock on the Hays County Courthouse, but that is one of the few differences.

The courthouse is constructed with a strong limestone base and the exterior walls are of tan brick. The dome and corner turrets are covered in copper.

The interior of the 1908 courthouse features a terrazzo floor with colorful mosaic tile flooring, including a Lone Star design, a marble and iron stairway, brick wainscoting and walnut paneling. The three floors open onto a rotunda. Many of the oak chairs and tables are extant and have been in use since the early 1900s.

WEBB COUNTY COURTHOUSE

Laredo. 1909
Alfred Giles. Architect

In the 1880s, Laredo was a sleepy little border town. There were only 40 or more Anglo Americans living in a population of 3,000 Mexicans. Most citizens, including many public officials, spoke no English, and legal pleadings and documents filed at the courthouse were written in both Spanish and English.[142] That changed when two railroads entered Laredo. American-designed buildings, including a new courthouse and city hall, were soon erected, streets were paved with gravel, a telephone exchange was installed and an English-speaking newspaper was published. By the end of the decade, the railroads had turned Laredo into a modern city. They had also created two sharply divided societies, one Anglo and one Mexican, which would define South Texas for generations.[143]

This is the third courthouse for the county, built in 1909, after the second courthouse was destroyed by fire. It is one of three twentieth-century courthouses designed by Alfred Giles and significantly departs from his previous works. Giles proved to be remarkably adaptable to the changing modes of design.

The building is in an unusual Renaissance Revival style. With its monumental arcade, it resembles a grand Mediterranean villa rather than a Texas courthouse. It features a red tile Mansard roof; the exterior walls are yellow brick with white stone trim.

The exterior is noted for its unified facades and a monumental arcade on the front elevation. The arcades work to protect the exterior walls. The second-floor balustrade adds to the building's charm. The strong corner pavilions with their red tile roofs and porthole windows are distinctive.

The interior of the building includes tile flooring and a stained glass window on the first floor landing. The wooden doors feature original beveled glass and brass door knobs. The three floors are connected by a wrought iron-trimmed staircase.

Over time, county leaders have enlarged the interior space by blocking the outer arcades on three sides and covering several porthole windows. Preservationists hope to restore the courthouse to its original proportions.

MASON COUNTY COURTHOUSE

Mason. 1909
Edward Columbus Hosford & Co. Architects

"Some ten miles brought me to the capital of Mason County. It is a site that is all beauty. It sits on a lofty prairie.... I was surprised at such architecture and such wealth of commerce.... In the midst of this attractiveness there is one harshness. The men, excepting those who live in the village, are walking arsenals. They bristle with pistols, blades and rifles and their heels clank with prodigious spurs.... Yet ... I heard no harsh voices and saw no demonstrative demeanor even in the drinking saloons.... They evidently solicit

no quarrels, but seem ever on the alert; and if a quarrel should arise, blood would flow.... The county of Mason has the most evil reputation in Texas for dark deeds."—Colonel N.A. Taylor, 1877[144]

Mason County is located in Central Texas, northwest of Austin in a region known as the Hill Country. Populated primarily by German immigrants, the county was organized in 1858. This Beaux Arts edifice was constructed in 1909 and serves as the county's third courthouse. The two previous courthouses were destroyed by fire.

This building features a center dome and clock tower. It is noteworthy for its four dominant gable front porticoes with two-story Doric columns. The second-floor windows are arched and frame the large two-story courtroom. The third floor of the building originally included a dormitory for the male jurors.

The rusticated stonework is complemented with contrasting sandstone lintels. Red sandstone is prevalent in the area and was used in most of the early commercial buildings in Mason.

HARRIS COUNTY

HARRIS COUNTY COURTHOUSE

Houston. 1910
Lang, Witchell & Barglebaugh. Architects

The struggle for voting rights in the South was long and difficult. White political leaders, with the active support of county officials, repeatedly placed impossible tests and restrictions on the right of black Americans to vote. Meeting at the Harris County Courthouse in 1934, the county's Democratic Party adopted a "Loyalty Rule" for primary elections. Voters would henceforth be required to present to election officials a poll tax payment receipt and prove under oath that they had voted for the Democratic ticket at least three times in the last six years. First-time voters were required to prove under oath that their parents had voted the straight Democratic ticket three times in the past six years.

Black leaders were mostly silent, but the editor of the *Houston Informer* said the new rule was an "obvious attempt to exclude negroes from voting, because negro citizens have had no opportunity to vote in recent years and are therefore unable to qualify." The editor of the *Houston Guide* said, "The negro is at the crossroads, where the radicals are beckoning to him. And yet he wants to be loyal to Democracy and its institutions."[145]

This Harris County Courthouse was completed in 1910. This rectangular structure is the fourth courthouse built on the site, which has been the courthouse square since Houston was founded in 1836. Charles Erwin Barglebaugh, an associate with the Dallas architectural firm of Lang & Witchell, designed this excellent

example of the Beaux Arts style with much of its ornamentation influenced by the Prairie School of Architecture. Earlier in his career, he worked under the tutelage of Frank Lloyd Wright.

The foundation is composed of rough-cut pink Texas granite; the exterior walls are of light brown St. Louis pressed brick. Corinthian columns frame the loggia bays and support the decorated pediments on each side. Sculptured eagles, lion heads and female faces are made of terra cotta, masonry and limestone. In 1938, county voters narrowly defeated a proposal to demolish their courthouse and build a more modern building.

Although worn and faded and in need of repair and restoration, the exterior still retains its essential character and well-proportioned design. In 1953, the building was significantly modified, and the interior bears little resemblance to the original master plan. A belated participant in the Texas Historic Courthouse Preservation Program, preservationists plan to return this stately building to its former grandeur.

JEFF DAVIS COUNTY COURTHOUSE

Fort Davis. 1910
Leslie L. Thurmon & Co. Architects

In 1941, Manuel Gonzales was a poor half-educated teenager from Fort Davis when America entered the war. Like most of his schoolmates, he enlisted in the Army and was assigned to the 36th Infantry Division. The "Texas Division" was an all-Texas unit with a distinctive T-patch as an insignia, and its foot soldiers were made up of boys from small towns across Texas. Popular with his comrades, Gonzales was promoted to be their platoon leader.

In the pre-dawn hours of September 9, 1943, Gonzales led his T-Patchers into a landing craft and headed for the beaches of Salerno Bay, Italy. In the first assault, they came under withering fire from German guns behind fortified defenses. Gonzales ordered his men to cover him as he made his way toward the German positions under heavy fire. He was shot in the chest, and his backpack was set on fire by tracer bullets, but he kept going. Crawling on his hands and knees close to the Germans, he tossed his grenades, knocking out the cannon that had the Texans pinned on the beach. For his bravery in World War II, Manuel Gonzales was awarded the Silver Star, the Distinguished Service Cross and the Purple Heart with Oak Leaf Cluster. His captain called him the, "best man that ever came to the regiment." Manuel Gonzales died from his wounds two years after the war ended. On Veterans Day of 1997, the citizens of Fort Davis dedicated a monument to his memory on the courthouse grounds.[146]

In 1880, in an attempt to discourage an effort by a few ranchers to move the county seat to Marfa, the political and business leaders of Fort Davis built a new courthouse and jail. It was an unadorned adobe building and was called the "bat cave courthouse." The nickname was in reference to its crude adobe jail. A jail cell had been carved out of solid rock under the floor of the sheriff's office to house prisoners. A trap door was placed over the opening of the dungeon and the only ventilation was from two small holes.[147] In spite of attempts to upgrade the jail, Marfa became the county seat in 1885. In 1887, Jeff Davis County was created, and Fort Davis was again designated a county seat.

The Beaux Arts clock tower features a four-sided Seth Thomas clock and a seven-hundred-pound bell, which was used as a fire alarm. Following the Mexican Revolution, it served as a warning signal of attacks by Mexican bandits.[148] It is still in use today.

This Classical Revival courthouse is made of concrete and rusticated pink stone. It features six imposing Doric columns guarding the front and rear recessed entrances. Restoration of the three-story structure included the reconstruction of its original 1910 balcony and the building's interior rooms and hallways. The courthouse and square have been restored, and the building was rededicated by state and local officials in 2003.

JONES COUNTY COURTHOUSE

Anson. 1910

Elmer George Withers. Architect

Anson Jones was a remarkable man. Like many early Texans he had suffered financial and professional ruin in the East and migrated to Texas in 1833 to start over. His medical practice flourished in Brazoria, and he became one of the leading advocates for independence from Mexico. When the revolution started in early 1836, Jones joined Houston's retreating army as a private and distinguished himself at the Battle of San Jacinto. Once Texas became a republic, he was elected to the Texas Congress; appointed minister to the United States and later secretary of state by Sam Houston; served in the Texas Senate; and in 1844 was elected as the third and last president of the Republic of Texas. Jones guided Texas into the Union and retired to Barrington, his plantation at Washington-on-the-Brazos. He hoped to be elected to the U.S. Senate, but was disheartened when Sam Houston and Thomas Jefferson Rusk were chosen instead. Having been passed over again for an open Senate seat in 1857, Jones became despondent and depressed. He committed suicide on a Houston city street in 1858.[149]

The county commissioners chose Elmer G. Withers to design their new courthouse. Withers was reared in the nearby small town of Stamford before opening his practice in Fort Worth. His design was a rectangular Beaux Arts style with Classical Revival details. The commissioners chose Pecos red sandstone and a light

orange-colored brick for the exterior, but left the actual design and its implementation to the architect.

The Jones County Courthouse is placed at the geometric center of Anson, and it has dominated the town since it was built in 1910. Standing firmly atop the tower, a Statue of Justice can be seen for miles across the West Texas prairie. The main entrance to this traditional Beaux Arts public building is framed by two imposing Ionic columns.

A statue, positioned at the center of the city and county that bear his name, portrays Anson Jones with a law book.

COOKE COUNTY COURTHOUSE

Gainesville. 1911

Otto H. Lang and Frank O. Witchell. Architects

In 1861, Cooke County and the surrounding counties along the Red River voted against secession, while the most of Texas voted overwhelmingly in favor of withdrawing from the Union. Emotions were high as many citizens remained loyal to the Union. When abolitionist leaders formed a Union League to pursue a new free state in North Texas, Texas state troops arrested more than 150 suspected traitors. In October of 1862, a "citizen's court" of twelve jurors was convened at the courthouse, and by a simple majority vote, many of the alleged insurrectionists were quickly tried and convicted. The court was in session for only 13 days, and by the time it adjourned, 41 men were hanged by order of the court or lynched by a mob in what would be known as "The Great Hanging at Gainesville."[150]

When Frank Lloyd Wright and Louis Sullivan introduced the Prairie School of design, they influenced architects across America in the same dramatic fashion as Henry Hobson Richardson had done in the previous century. It was a revolutionary departure from past traditions. Designed by the Dallas firm of Lang & Witchell, the Cooke County Courthouse is one of three Beaux Arts-designed courthouses in Texas to utilize strong elements of the Prairie School. It is the fourth courthouse to occupy the site.

Buff-colored brick and locally quarried limestone cover the exterior of this three-story, cruciform-plan structure. The bays of the second- and third-floor windows are divided by two-story limestone Ionic columns. A parapet wall features terra cotta symbols of justice above each entrance. Below the parapet, a cornice encircles the courthouse.

The courthouse features a copper-clad dome with pinnacle, glazed terra cotta ornamentation and eagle brackets. In 1920, clocks were added to the dome as a World War I memorial.

In the Sullivan-inspired interior is a tall central atrium with a beautiful stained glass skylight under the tower. While many of the interior spaces have been altered over time, the square atrium is extant. Black and white marble ornamentation and terrazzo floors enhance the interior's splendor. This is the fourth courthouse built for the county on the same site in the county seat of Gainesville. Local preservationists and county leaders are currently planning to completely restore the handsome building with the financial assistance and expertise provided by the Texas Historic Courthouse Preservation Program.

WILLIAMSON COUNTY

WILLIAMSON COUNTY COURTHOUSE

Georgetown. 1911
Charles Henry Page & Brother. Architects

I n 1848, the Texas Legislature, in response to a formal petition of local citizens, established Williamson County, carving it out of western Milam County. They named the new county after Robert M. Williamson, a newspaper editor, veteran of the Battle of San Jacinto, Texas Ranger, schoolteacher, legislator and judge. The First Congress of Texas elected him to a judgeship of the First District Court, which under the existing law made him a member of the Texas Supreme Court. He held proceedings under a giant oak tree on the Colorado County public square until a courthouse could be built. Judge Williamson was well known for another reason. An early illness had left his right leg permanently pulled back at the knee, leaving his foot forever hanging in the air. He wore a wooden leg and gained the nickname of "Three Legged Willie." During the early years of the Republic, Judge Williamson became a celebrity as a skilled orator and raconteur. He wore his peg leg and his sobriquet with great distinction.[151]

The Williamson County Courthouse of 1877 was razed in 1910 to make room on the courthouse square for the present structure, which is located in the well-preserved central historic district of Georgetown. The exterior walls of this Beaux Arts building are of beige brick with white limestone trim. On each side of the building is a central pavilion with four Ionic columns. A four-sided clock and a Statue of Justice are placed on the handsome copper

dome. It had beautifully carved marble pediments above each entrance, with the roofline encircled by a balustrade.

The structure was dramatically altered in 1965, when a few of the baluster railings became loose, and county leaders ordered the balustrade and the elaborate marble pediments removed.[152] The unadorned brickwork replaced them, and as a result, the building lost much of its original elegance.

In January of 2006, with assistance from the Texas Historical Commission, county leaders commenced an ambitious restoration project that will return the structure to its 1911 appearance. The brick parapet around the top of the building will be replaced with the original balustrades and triangular pediments.

SAN SABA COUNTY COURTHOUSE

San Saba. 1911

Walter Chamberlin & Co. Architects

"**S**am Huston. Govnr.... I have bin reelected to the office of Assessor and Collector of Sansaba County ... Send me a SixShooter of the largest size and Buoy knife.—E. Estep."[153]

Until the later part of the 1800s, most county officials were ill-suited to maintain law and order in frontier towns, and when local law enforcement could not keep the peace, county leaders would petition the governor to send the Texas Rangers to restore order. There was very little law in the small towns along the San Saba River. In the spring of 1878, the county judge wrote in desperation: "The lives of the officers of the San Saba County are hanging by a thread."

Ranger Captain George Arrington, known as "Arrington the Iron Handed," was ordered to proceed with speed to San Saba to protect an attorney who had killed a saloon keeper over a local option election. With ten Rangers, Arrington made a forced march through the night and arrived at San Saba by dawn. "I ... found the entire community in a great state of excitement and a mob nearly ready to do their dirty work ... I am camped in the courthouse and have no fears of being attacked."[154]

San Saba County was organized in 1856, and the first courthouse was completed a year later. It served as a school and a meeting house until it was replaced in 1878. Built in 1911, this is the county's third courthouse. The structure, in an eclectic style known as Texas Renaissance, reflects not only the changing tastes in public architecture in the early years of the twentieth century, but also a more practical need for functional space and an economy of construction.

ATASCOSA COUNTY

ATASCOSA COUNTY COURTHOUSE

Jourdanton. 1912
Henry Truman Phelps. Architect

Atascosa County is located on the remote South Texas Plains along the Atascosa River. The region was first settled in 1828 by Jose Antonio Navarro pursuant to a land grant from Mexico that was later acknowledged by the State of Texas. In 1857, when the county was first organized, Navarro donated land for a county seat that he named Navatasco. A log courthouse was built, but within a year, because of Indian raids, the county seat was moved to Pleasonton. A new courthouse cost $125, and for a jail, county officials dug a twelve-foot deep hole covered by a padlocked trap door. In 1909, businessman Jourdan Campbell founded a new town within a few miles of Pleasonton in a successful effort to lure the Artesian Belt Railroad across his land. Within a year, Jourdanton became the county seat.[155]

San Antonio architect Henry T. Phelps employed the Beaux Arts Classic style in all of his civic buildings except for this unique building for Atascosa County. It is the only surviving county courthouse in Texas utilizing the Mission Revival style. The Hidalgo County Courthouse, built in 1908, was an almost identical structure but was razed by county leaders in the 1950s to build a more modern building.

The dark reddish-brown brick building with its cast stone arches and stringcourses features prominent corner pavilions and  three-story towers. The basement walls are made of concrete that has been covered in plaster to resemble limestone. The first floor is encircled by an arcaded loggia, which was originally open and then closed in the 1920s to gain more office space. A relatively short central tower with two arched windows on each side rises from the hipped terra cotta tiled roof. The structure's ornamentation is strongly influenced by the work of Louis Sullivan.

Mission Revival was never a popular style for public buildings in Texas, and the Atascosa County Courthouse stands alone in the state as an important architectural icon. In 2003, the courthouse was restored and rededicated as part of the Texas Historic Courthouse Preservation Program.

CAMERON COUNTY COURTHOUSE

Brownsville. 1912
Atlee Bernard Ayres. Architect

Charles Stillman was born in Connecticut, the educated son of a wealthy New England merchant. In 1828, he traveled to Matamoros to establish part of his father's trading business. Stillman was a brilliant businessman and an adroit politician. He organized a land company and sold lots to develop the new town named Brownsville, which under his leadership became the county seat and the most dominant city of the Rio Grande Valley. During the Mexican War, Stillman ferried American troops across the border, and during the Civil War, he transported Confederate cotton to Mexico. He profited from both conflicts. By 1865, Stillman was one of the most powerful leaders in South Texas and one of the richest men in America.[156]

This excellent Classical Revival building is one of renowned San Antonio architect Atlee Ayres' best courthouses. The exterior of the three-story structure is understated and relatively unadorned. The walls are covered in brown brick, and encircling the structure are brick pilasters with terra cotta Corinthian capitals. Without a dominant central tower or dome, and with its flat roof and little ornamentation, the understated building could easily be unrecognizable as a governmental building. To announce its purpose, inscribed on a cast terra cotta shield above each entrance is "1912," and "Cameron County Courthouse" is carved on the frieze.

Ayers utilized the majestic designs of Louis Sullivan for the

interior. The first-floor hallways lead from each entrance to an octagonal rotunda. A large chandelier hangs from the stained glass dome over the rotunda that is decorated with plaster ribs. It is one of the most beautiful interiors of any courthouse in the state.

As a result of funding from the Texas Historic Courthouse Preservation Program, a major preservation effort will completely restore the building, including returning the commissioner's court to its original double-height district courtroom. This is the second courthouse for Cameron County. It was replaced by a new courthouse in 1981 but has been faithfully preserved by county leaders.

FRANKLIN COUNTY COURTHOUSE

Mount Vernon. 1912

Leslie L. Thurmon & Co. Architects

In 1875, an election was ordered to determine the location of the county seat for Franklin County, and three sites were placed on the ballot. The campaign was spirited. Each community posted how much land and money they would offer for a new courthouse. A few days before the election, heavy spring rains flooded the creeks and river crossings making turnout critical. Supporters of Mount Vernon took no chances and quickly built a boat to ferry their registered voters to the polling places. More importantly, Mount Vernon supporters staged horse races on Election Day, assuring that most men and boys of voting age would come to town regardless of the high water. Some prospective voters swam the swollen creeks to get to the race track. Mount Vernon won by a large majority.[157]

This well-proportioned, Neo-Classical Revival building was designed by L.L. Thurmon of Dallas. Unlike most county seats, the Franklin County Courthouse is not placed on the town square, but faces it. The first courthouse for the county was located at the center of the square.

The large porticoed entrances on each side of the building have four prominent Doric columns supporting an unadorned pediment. A four-sided, domed clock tower serves the people of Mount Vernon. Like many historic public buildings in the state, the interior has been altered to accommodate additional space for county employees. The courthouse is in need of repair and restoration.

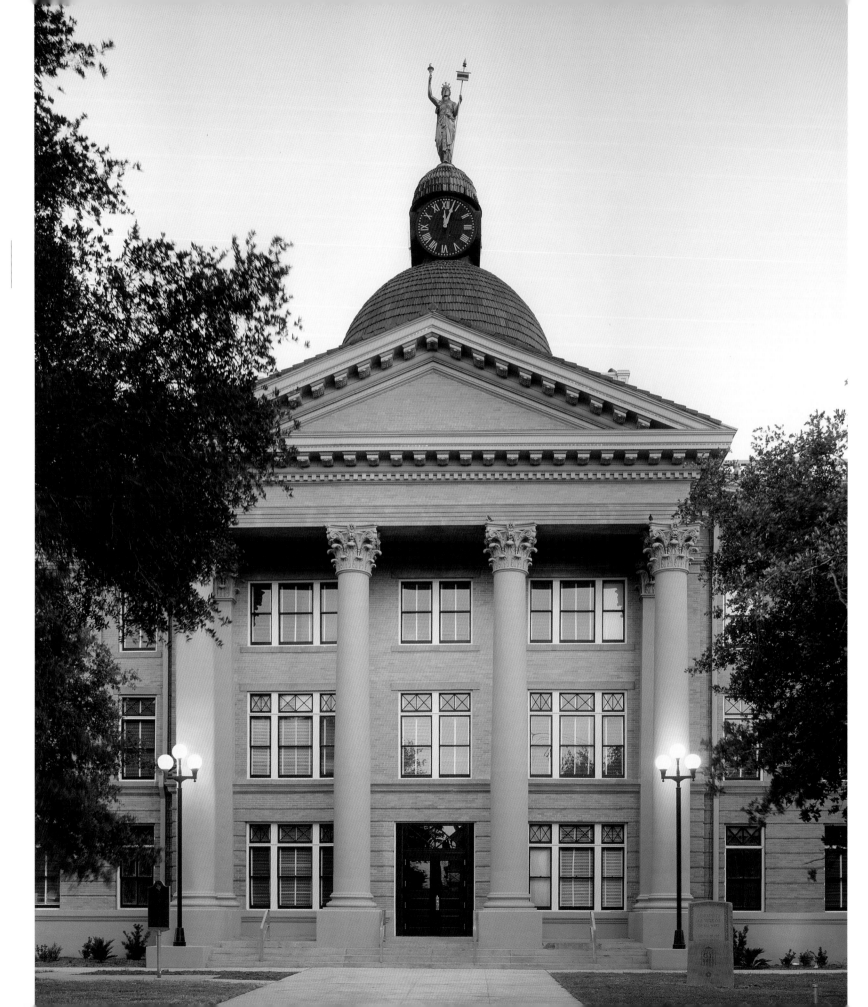

BEE COUNTY COURTHOUSE

Beeville. 1912
Stephenson & Heldenfels. Architects

Bee County was officially organized in 1858 on 550,000 acres of land carved from five neighboring counties. The first county court was held under a tree on the banks of the Medio Creek at Marysville, a town site named after a girl who had been murdered by Indians. The courthouse was made of wooden pickets with a dirt floor, and the furniture consisted of a table and two benches. When the court was called into session, every able-bodied man in the county packed food and a change of clothes in a blanket tied to the back of his saddle, rode to Marysville and stayed until the court adjourned. There were so few men in the county it took all of them to hold court.[158]

Designed by local architect William C. Stephenson, this three-story Beaux Arts building is the third courthouse for Bee County. The structure is supported by a raised concrete foundation, and tan-colored brick was used for the exterior. On each side of the building, two-story brick pilasters frame the entrances. The second and third floors are enhanced by two-story pilasters that break the three horizontal cast stone bands that encircle the building.

The main entrance to the courthouse is through a powerful three-story projecting portico with four massive Corinthian columns.

The hipped roof and dome are covered with distinctive red clay tile. The central dome is constructed in an unusual beehive design. Standing above the four-sided clock is the Goddess of Justice holding a torch of knowledge and a staff with the scroll of records.

In 1941, an addition was added to one side of the building, and in 1949, the interior of the courthouse was significantly remodeled. County leaders have chosen to participate in the Texas Historic Courthouse Preservation Program and plan to restore the aging structure.

HENDERSON COUNTY COURTHOUSE

Athens. 1913

Leslie L. Thurmon & Co. Architects

In 1850, area leaders agreed to establish their new county seat at the center of the county and name the town after Athens, Greece. Lots were sectioned off, including a square for a courthouse. Six weeks before the first wooden courthouse was built, District Judge Oran Milo Roberts held the first district court session under a large red oak tree on the square. The minutes recorded his opening remarks: "This court is held under the shade  of an oak tree … which public authorities of Athens are requested to preserve as a memorial to the habits of early Texans." Roberts would later serve as the chief justice of the Texas Supreme Court and two terms as governor. In 1886, a fire destroyed the courthouse and the old oak tree. Citizens carved a cane from the remains of the tree and delivered it to Governor Roberts in a ceremony before the Texas Supreme Court in Austin.[159]

This four-story Classical Revival courthouse by L.L. Thurmon is made of reddish-brown brick, concrete and stone. The courthouse is uniquely designed with four bays projecting from each corner of the central block. A central dome and four three-bay pedimented entries with Doric columns are distinctive elements of the structure. A decorated pediment and the name of the county carved in stone announce the building's purpose.

JOHNSON COUNTY COURTHOUSE

Cleburne. 1913

Otto H. Lang and Frank O. Witchell. Architects

"Johnson County Courthouse Destroyed by Fire—Building Takes Fire in Tower From Unknown Causes and Consumed in Three Hours—City Marshal A. Bledsoe is Caught Under Falling Tin and Brick and is Roasted to Death—Body Recovered With Hands Still Holding Nozzle—Funeral at 3 O'clock This Afternoon"—The Cleburne Morning Review, 1912.[160]

On the night of April 15, 1912, when the fire marshal and night watchmen first saw the flames, they raced to the county square firing their six-shooters to sound the alarm. Before the fire wagons arrived, the flames were sweeping downward from the tower. The citizens of Cleburne watched as their elegant courthouse was quickly destroyed. Fire Chief Baylor Bledsoe was out of town, and his brother, Abe Bledsoe, took his place. Taking command on the second floor, he was killed fighting the fire. The following afternoon Cleburne businesses were closed during the funeral to honor their fallen hero.[161]

This 1913 Classical courthouse, designed by the architectural firm of Lang & Witchell, is heavily influenced by the Prairie School. It is similar to the impressive courthouse the firm designed for Cooke County two years earlier. Both courthouses rank among the best examples of the period, combining traditional Beaux Arts influences and features of the Prairie School.

While the structure is in many respects conventional, the exterior of the courthouse has Prairie School ornamentation, including stylized capitals and pendants to mark its adaptation of a style that had a significant impact on popular tastes across the country. The six-story clock tower is one of the grand building's most important features.

It is the building's interior that is most significant. Four main corridors are joined in a central lobby, which rises six stories. The atrium is decorated with Sullivan-themed foliated detailing and marble walls. The outstanding stained glass dome is one of the most beautiful in the state, with its exquisite details, including four state seals.

The Texas red granite was from Burnet County, the dark marble was from Georgia and the white stone was shipped from Indiana. The bricks were made in the nearby small town of Elgin. This is the sixth county courthouse for Johnson County, which was organized in 1854.

ANDERSON COUNTY COURTHOUSE

Palestine. 1914
Charles Henry Page and Brother. Architects

Percy Wynne had been indicted for the burglary of Abe Hort's pool hall. The evidence of his crime and the court's records were stored in the Anderson County Courthouse awaiting his trial. Wynne concluded that the only way to beat the indictment was to burn down the courthouse and destroy the incriminating papers. In the early morning hours of January, 1912, the defendant broke into the building and set the blaze. W.C. Dodson had designed the elaborately detailed structure in 1885, with a four-story red brick tower. It was quickly gutted by the fire. Percy Wynne was sentenced to ten years in prison for his crime and county commissioners quickly ordered the design and construction of a new courthouse.[162]

Located on a hilltop courthouse square, this powerful structure dominates the town below. Court proceedings were held under a stand of oak trees on the corner of the courthouse square until the first courthouse was erected in 1847.[163] The present building is the fourth courthouse on this site.

Designed by the Austin-based Page brothers, this stately Beaux Arts building features four equally powerful projecting porticoes with large Corinthian columns supporting pediments on each facade. The porticoes are connected by a balustrade. The stone trim and Corinthian pilasters encircle the structure and add contrast to the terra cotta-colored brick exterior. The centrally

positioned dome is topped by a Statue of Justice overlooking the county seat of Palestine. This beautifully proportioned courthouse is one of the most outstanding public buildings of the era.

KLEBERG COUNTY COURTHOUSE

Kingsville. 1914
Atlee Bernard Ayres. Architect

At the turn of the century, Robert Kleberg, a lawyer raised and educated in Virginia, ran the 825,000-acre King Ranch that dominated South Texas. Married to Richard and Henrietta King's daughter Alice, he was the ruler of a vast empire of rangeland and cattle. Only one thing was scarce on the Rio Grande plains—water. Kleberg needed it, but not just for his Longhorns. He knew that only a dependable source of water would bring the railroads to South Texas, and only the railroads could connect South Texas to the rest of the world. His ranch hands drilled and dynamited the rangeland, and when his cowboys finally struck water, the railroads came. Kleberg built a town in a pasture twenty miles from his ranch house and named it after his father-in-law. In 1913, the Legislature organized Kleberg County with Kingsville as the county seat.[164]

During the period, this handsome Classical brick building was a popular design in a number of newly created Texas counties.[165] This fine courthouse, designed by the accomplished architect Atlee Ayres, is understated and relatively unadorned when compared to most of his other public buildings. Based in San Antonio, Ayres would design several South Texas courthouses.

Two columns frame the porch entrance and support a decorated parapet, which announces the building's purpose. The brackets under the cornice and the details on the portico are noteworthy. The brick and stone structure is the only courthouse built for Kleberg County.

BROOKS COUNTY COURTHOUSE

Falfurrias. 1914
Alfred Giles. Architect

In South Texas, the creation of new counties was about much more than population growth; it was about raw political power between the old guard ranching interests and their Mexican allies versus a new generation of farmers. Ed C. Lasater was a wealthy and influential Republican. In 1910, his continued efforts to beat the machine politicians of Starr County were finally successful, and the Legislature created Brooks County. Lasater wasted no time in selling farm tracts to farmers from the Midwest. The results were extraordinary. In 1906, Falfurrias was a 400,000-acre cattle ranch with fewer than 200 people. By 1920, Lasater had sold more than 60,000 acres of his 360,000-acre ranch, and Falfurrias had a population of 2,500 citizens.[166]

This Classical Revival brick and stone courthouse was designed by the great Alfred Giles. It is one of the three twentieth century county courthouses designed by Giles that reflect his sensitive adaptation to the changing modes of popular design.

It utilizes a colonnade of Corinthian columns that supports a

large cornice in front of the building. A second-floor balcony divides the columnar entrance. The balcony is repeated on the rear of the building, decorated with arched second-floor windows.

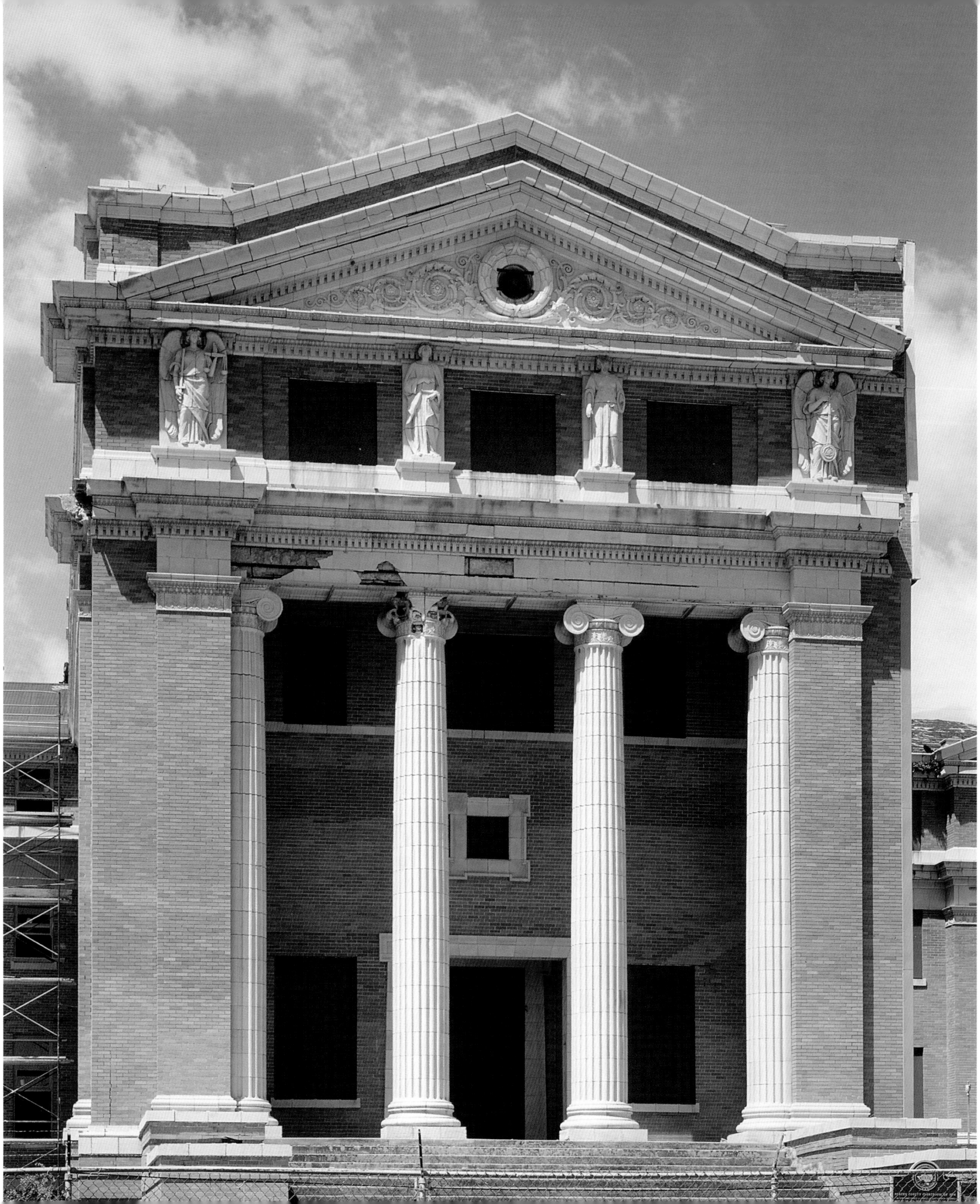

NUECES COUNTY COURTHOUSE

Corpus Christi. 1914
Harvey Lindsley Page. Architect

Colonel Henry L. Kinney was a fearless and smart merchant and one of the founders of Corpus Christi. In 1839, he established a trading post and built his Rancho on the west shore of Corpus Christi Bay. Kinney traded with everyone—Indians, Mexicans and Texans. He was accused of treason in 1845 for giving assistance to the enemy, but he and his partner were acquitted. Kinney's defense was that he had to sacrifice his political beliefs and principals to survive: "… when Mr. Mexican came, I treated him with a great deal of politeness … when Mr. American came, I did the same with him … when Mr. Indian came I was disposed to compromise with him." Kinney prospered.[167] He sold the county three lots for $300 to build the first courthouse.

This stately Beaux Arts edifice, designed by Washington, D.C., architect Harvey L. Page, is one of a kind in Texas.[168] Completed in 1914 at a cost of $250,000, it stands six stories and is positioned on a hill overlooking Corpus Christi. County commissioners designated this site for their courthouse in 1853. One of the oldest buildings in the city, this is one of the most important architectural treasures in Texas.

This noble courthouse is built of gray pressed brick and trimmed with white terra cotta. The original roof was made with red tile. The main entrance to the courthouse is located on the second floor and is reached by a wide stairway. The projecting entrance of

the central pavilion is dramatically marked by large two-story Ionic columns supporting an entablature. Four carved figures stand above the cornice. A small circular window is centered on the decorated pediment.

The T-shaped building has four-story pavilions placed at each end of the two wings. The wings are designated by smaller two-story columnar porches and pediments. The result is a significant and unique edifice that makes a powerful statement of public purpose.

Courtrooms and county offices were on the first four floors, and the top two floors served as a jail. Small apartments were provided for the jailer and court officials on the upper floors. Families of the court personnel resided in the building through the 1950s. During devastating hurricanes in 1919 and 1961, citizens took refuge in the reinforced steel structure. Poorly planned additions that were added in the 1930s and 1960s have greatly diminished the integrity of the building's original design. Today it stands vacant, undergoing a major restoration effort that will include removing the incongruent additions.

TRINITY COUNTY COURTHOUSE

Groveton. 1914
L.S. Green and Charles Henry Page and Brother. Architects

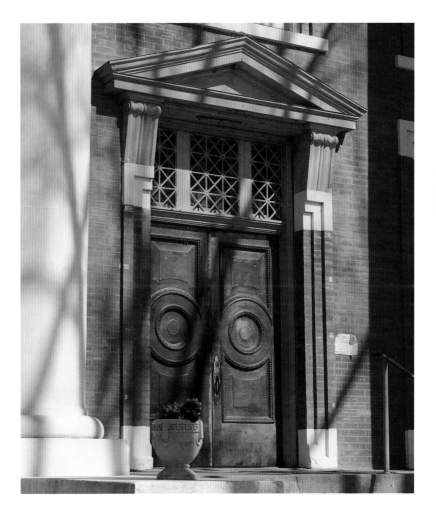

When Trinity County was created in 1850 by the Texas Legislature, the settlement of Sumpter, located within five miles of the center of the county, was declared the county seat. Deep in East Texas, the county's economy was based largely on farming, with several large slaveholders dominating the economic and political interests of the county. When the Great Northern Railway ran its tracks through the small hamlet of Trinity in 1872, the county changed almost overnight. The courthouse in Sumpter was destroyed by fire, but the center of the county's economy had already shifted to Trinity, which was declared the county seat 1873. The next year Pennington became the seat of government, and the records were moved once again into a new courthouse, which burned to the ground in 1876. The area's old growth timber, which was plentiful, became a cash crop, and sawmill towns were built near the railroad lines. In 1882, the company town of Groveton was chosen as the fourth county seat of Trinity County.[169]

This three-story Classical Revival courthouse is made of a cast-in-place concrete foundation painted white, with bright red-faced brick and white trim. It is the fifth courthouse for Trinity County. The top floor of the old building originally served as a dormitory for the male jurors who traveled from the outreaches of the county.

In 1908, L.S. Green designed a free-standing annex adjacent to the main courthouse that was known as the records vault. When C.H. Page designed the current building in 1914, he joined the annex to the main building and carefully matched the earlier style.

The courthouse has a three-story central hall with a two-story wing on each side. The three sections are appropriately connected to become one continuous building. Three entrances are on both sides of the structure, with the main entrance designated by a large portico with four large columns and pilasters. The large copper-clad doors are extant.

The 1914 courthouse and the adjoining square were listed on the National Register of Historic Places in 2003. The structure is currently in poor condition and in need of repair and restoration. In 2003, the Texas Historical Commission awarded the county a planning grant to initiate the proper restoration of the stately old building. The cost of repair and restoration may reach $4 million.

VAL VERDE COUNTY

VAL VERDE COUNTY COURTHOUSE

Del Rio. 1887/1915

Jacob L. Larmour & Arthur Osborn Watson/Atlee Bernard Ayres. Architects

I n 1885, Val Verde County was officially organized. The county stretched for 3,242 square miles along the Rio Grande, three times the size of Rhode Island. In the county's first election, Roy Bean was elected Justice of the Peace in Langtry, an isolated little town 400 miles east of El Paso. Judge Bean was not an attorney and had no formal training as a judge. His courtroom was in one corner of his Jersey Lilly Saloon, which he called the "Law West of the Pecos." Bean constantly frustrated county officials with his contrary brand of justice. In 1896, prize fighting was a felony in Texas, and when promoters were denied permission to stage a world championship heavy-weight fight in El Paso, Judge Bean offered to stage the match on a sand bar in the middle of the Rio Grande near Langtry. Trains of spectators traveled from across the state to watch the fight from the high bluffs on the Texas side of the river. Thirty Texas Rangers joined the crowd to keep order and ensure the fight was not on Texas soil. A quick knockout ended the match in the first round, and the fans retired to the judge's saloon.[170]

Val Verde County was organized in 1885 and named for a Civil War battle in New Mexico. When originally constructed in 1887, the courthouse was an elaborate Second Empire building with convex mansard and conical roofs above the four octagonal corner towers. In 1915, county leaders commissioned architect Atlee B. Ayres

to enlarge and substantially change the character of the building. The statues and towers were removed and a third floor was added. The building retains many of its original features, including the main entrance. The exterior walls are made of rough-faced limestone punctuated by a smooth stone stringcourse. The paired pilasters are decorated with geometric designs. According to local legend, the stonework was done by Native American masons.

Working with the Texas Historical Commission, preservationists and local officials have faithfully restored the old limestone courthouse to its 1915 configuration. The only courthouse for Val Verde County, the building was officially rededicated in 2004.[171]

BLANCO COUNTY COURTHOUSE

Johnson City. 1916
Henry Truman Phelps. Architect

In 1858, the land along the Pedernales and the Blanco rivers was still a wilderness. A day's ride west from Austin was the difference between civilization and the frontier. Not many men and only a few women tried to settle there, not because of the land, which was plentiful, but because of fear. This was Comanche and Kiowa territory, and to settle on their sacred land was fraught with danger. Many Hill Country families met horrible torture and painful deaths at the hands of the Comanches. Women were raped then killed, and many victims were scalped alive. Between 1836 and 1860, hundreds of men, women and children were killed or carried off. The warriors were better horsemen than the settlers, and against a single shot rifle, their arrows were far deadlier.[172] But families did come to settle the land close to the two rivers, and by 1858, enough of them were there to petition the State Legislature to become a new county. Blanco County and the county seat of Blanco were named after the white limestone that was so prevalent throughout the Hill Country. They built a church, a school and a courthouse. And for almost twenty years, they fought the Indians to survive.[173]

This is the third county courthouse for Blanco County. It was designed by Henry T. Phelps in a Classical Revival style and built in 1916, when Johnson City became the county seat. The county's 1885 courthouse was designed by F.E. Ruffini in his patented Second Empire style. It still stands in Blanco.

Doric columns support the formal triangular pediments on the four facades of the sturdy structure. Like most commercial buildings in the Hill Country, the exterior walls of the building are constructed with native limestone.

Much less dramatic than many courthouses of the era with their large domes and towers, a small dome is placed at the center of this rectangular building. Multiple tall two-over-two windows allowed ventilation during the hot Hill Country summers.

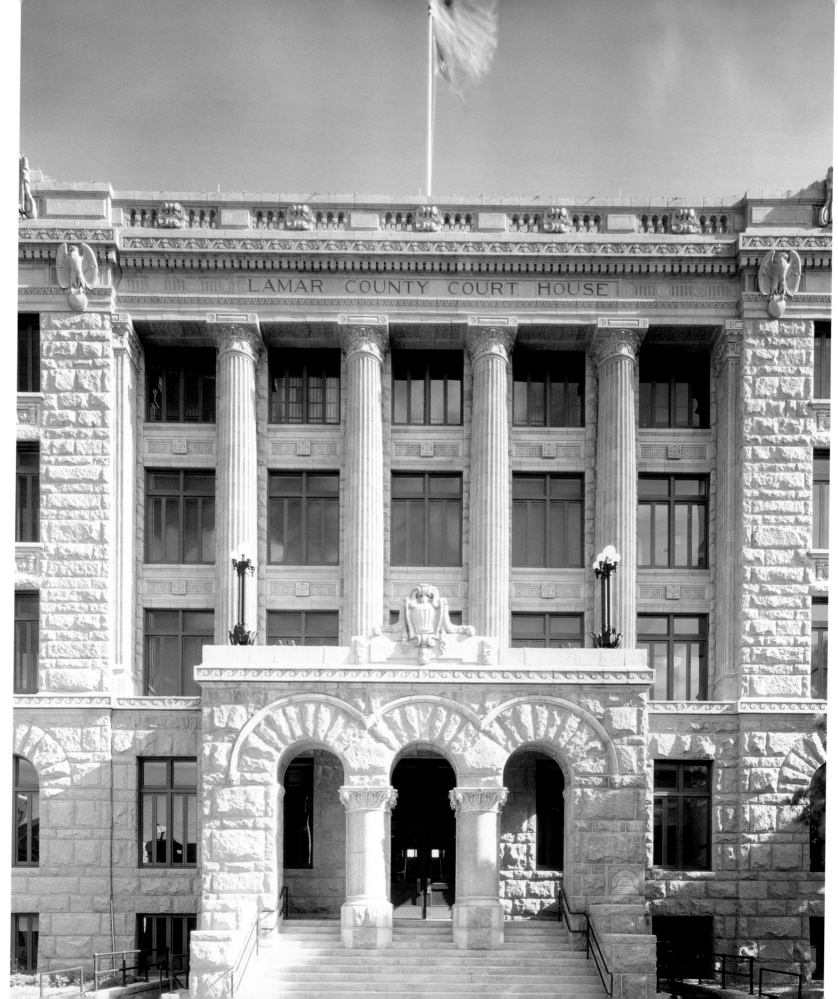

LAMAR COUNTY COURTHOUSE

Paris. 1917
Sanguinet & Staats. Architects

Founded by the Fifth Congress of the Republic of Texas in 1841, Lamar County in the Red River Valley is one of the oldest county governments in Texas. It was named after the Republic's second president, Mirabeau Buonaparte Lamar. The first county seat was established in the small settlement of Lafayette in 1841. When in 1842, the Texas Congress passed a law requiring the county seat to be within five miles of the center of a county, the county records were transferred to Mount Vernon, but a courthouse was never built. A local landowner offered fifty acres in a small settlement known as Pinhook but later named after Paris, France. It became the final county seat in 1844.[174]

This is the county's sixth courthouse. It is a solid building built with the same color and textured granite that was used in the State Capitol in Austin. The structure is a Classical Revival design with strong Romanesque features. It is built on the original foundation of the previous courthouse, which was destroyed when a fire ravaged the town of Paris in 1916.

Heavy engaged granite columns support triple-arched porticoes. The upper floors feature three-story half-columns supporting a cornice that is festooned with terra cotta medallions and eagles.

A complete restoration of this courthouse has been completed, which included removing the dropped ceilings and returning the original district courtroom and its second-floor balcony to their original condition. The building was officially rededicated by county and state leaders in 2005.

FREESTONE COUNTY

FREESTONE COUNTY COURTHOUSE

Fairfield. 1919
W.R. Kaufman and Atlee B. Ayers. Architects

One year after the young men left Freestone County to join the Confederate army, they invaded New Mexico Territory and fought heroically at the Battle of Val Verde, near Santa Fe.[175] Having captured several Union cannon, they were nicknamed the Val Verde Battery. The unit brought their artillery back to Texas and later fought engagements in Louisiana capturing more cannon from the Federals. When the Rebels prepared to surrender at the end of the war, they had no intention of giving up their guns. They brought them back to Freestone County and buried them. In 1885, when Democrat Grover Cleveland won the presidency, the veterans of the Val Verde Battery exhumed their cannon, fired them in salute to the new president and proudly placed one on the courthouse square where it remains today.[176]

This Classical Revival courthouse, the fourth for Freestone County, is a fine example of a popular style during the period. Its exterior walls are made of tan brick contrasted with a light terra cotta ornamentation and trim.

The basement floor is a half-story below ground, with the main floor accessible by a flight of stairs. Four two-story Ionic  columns guard the facades, while two matching columns are placed at each end of the building. A pronounced cornice encircles the structure. Rather than a dome or tower, the edifice is crowned by a parapet.

HUDSPETH COUNTY COURTHOUSE

Sierra Blanca. 1920
Buetell & Hardie. Architects

In the mid-1870s, disputes over the legal rights to the large salt deposits at the foot of Guadalupe Peak erupted into violence. The "Salt War" was a bloody political and economic fight between Anglo businessmen led by District Judge Charles Howard and State Representative Don Louis Cardis, the leader of the Mexican opposition. Mexicans and Texans had freely loaded their wagons with salt for generations, but Howard saw a profit in gaining title to the lands and charging fees for the salt. The debate turned deadly when the judge gunned down Cardis. Armed followers of Cardis surrounded Howard and his men, capturing and then executing them. Members of the Texas Congressional delegation, at the request of the governor, investigated the killings, but no significant action was taken, except to ensure that Fort Bliss would become a permanent military post. The Salt War was over.[177]

Hudspeth County was created from El Paso County in 1917, and the courthouse was completed in 1920. Designed by El Paso architect Bradford Hardie, this is the only adobe courthouse in Texas, as well as the only Spanish Colonial Revival county courthouse constructed in the state.[178] It is a special and unique approach to public architecture in Texas.

This single-story courthouse has eighteen-inch-thick exterior walls constructed of adobe brick and covered with painted stucco.

The 18x24-inch adobe bricks were made on the courthouse square. The low hipped roof is made of red Spanish tile. The smooth exterior is broken by a central arched entryway with the name of the county and an eagle and wreath carved in stone. The interior rooms have fifteen-foot ceilings.

The courthouse is still in use and has undergone a major restoration project, including reinforcing the solid exterior walls. The building has been returned to its 1920s condition and was rededicated in 2004.

DALLAM COUNTY COURTHOUSE

Dalhart. 1923
Smith & Townes. Architects

Dallam County is located on the High Plains in the far northwestern corner of the Texas Panhandle. With a population of 119, the county was created in 1890 and named after James W. Dallam, an early Republic of Texas lawyer and newspaper editor. Texline was named county seat because of its proximity to the rail line. Ten years later, Twist Junction was created at a new rail crossing. No one was pleased with the name, so after combining the first syllables of the names of two railroad companies, the town was called Denrock. That name proved unpopular as well. Ten county leaders were each asked to submit ten names for consideration. Finally, Ora Atkinson took the names of Dallam and Hartley counties and made every possible spelling combination until Dalhart was chosen. County voters responded favorably by voting to move the county seat to Dalhart in 1903.[179]

This Classical Revival courthouse, the county's third, was designed by the Amarillo firm of Smith & Townes. It is a fine example of a style popular during the 1920s that was repeated in several courthouses, including those in Freestone, Lubbock, Lynn and Fairfield counties.

This three-story courthouse is constructed with red brick and cream-colored stone detailing. It is built on a rectangular plan with a flat roof instead of a tower or dome. A half-basement is surmounted by stone stairs leading to the main floor. A stone watercourse encircles the basement and a stone stringcourse encircles the building above the second-floor windows.

Four Ionic columns stand two-stories tall and support the projecting portico of the building's central entrance. The third floor is positioned above the denticulated stone cornice and is surmounted by a stepped parapet.

The facades at each end of the courthouse are similar to the front facade, but smaller, with a two-story projecting portico supported by Ionic columns and topped with the entablature that encircles the structure.

SCHLEICHER COUNTY COURTHOUSE

Eldorado. 1924

Henry Truman Phelps. Architect

I n 1901, the first courthouse for Schleicher County was built at the center of the public square in Eldorado. It was a two-story wooden frame building that soon proved inadequate for the growing county. Badly in need of repairs and in dangerously poor condition, county leaders urged citizens to support a bond election in 1917 to pay for a new stone courthouse. When the votes were counted at the courthouse, the proposal failed. That night, the old building mysteriously caught fire and burned to the ground, making a new courthouse a necessity. Another election was quickly called, and this time, the women of the county were invited to vote. The bonds for the new courthouse were approved. County commissioners offered a $500 reward for the arrest and conviction of the arsonist, but no one was ever brought to justice. [180]

Schleicher County is located in the Edwards Plateau of Southwest Texas. It was organized in 1887, but because the population was scarce, it was not until 1901 that citizens elected their first county officials.

Prominent San Antonio architect Henry T. Phelps designed this solid Classical Revival courthouse. Construction was completed in 1924. Phelps was talented and inventive. His two other public buildings in Atascosa and Blanco counties reflect the wide range of his designs.

A large entablature and parapet are supported by four Doric columns, guarding the entrance to the county's most important building.

Intent on constructing a building that would stand the test of time, local leaders used native limestone from local quarries. Smooth stone lintels and a belt course frame the windows and mark the three-story structure, contrasting with the rusticated stone walls.

WHEELER COUNTY COURTHOUSE

Wheeler. 1925
E.H. Eades. Architect

"... a trading post started near Fort Elliott where an immense buffalo hide trading was done, many thousand buffalos being sold annually. It was patronized by outlaws, thieves, cutthroats and buffalo hunters, with a large percent of prostitutes. Taking it all in, I think it was the hardest place I ever saw on the frontier except for Cheyenne, Wyoming.... There was no semblance of law in this part of the Panhandle except what was enforced by the cattlemen arbitrarily.... Now in 1878 the conglomeration of buffalo hunters, gamblers, thieves and thugs conceived the idea of organizing Wheeler County.... there were a few genuinely good men who afterwards became settlers."— Rancher Charles Goodnight[181]

Architect E.H. Eades of Shamrock designed this Classical Revival courthouse, completed in 1925. Corner pavilions frame the front of this relatively unadorned structure. The three-story projecting portico and four Ionic columns give the building its sense of purpose. Five arched windows on the second floor are part of the structure's modest decoration.

The building was faithfully restored and rededicated in 2004,  including restoring the balcony and original furnishings in the large district courtroom. This is the third courthouse for Wheeler County, which in 1879 became the first organized county in the Panhandle.

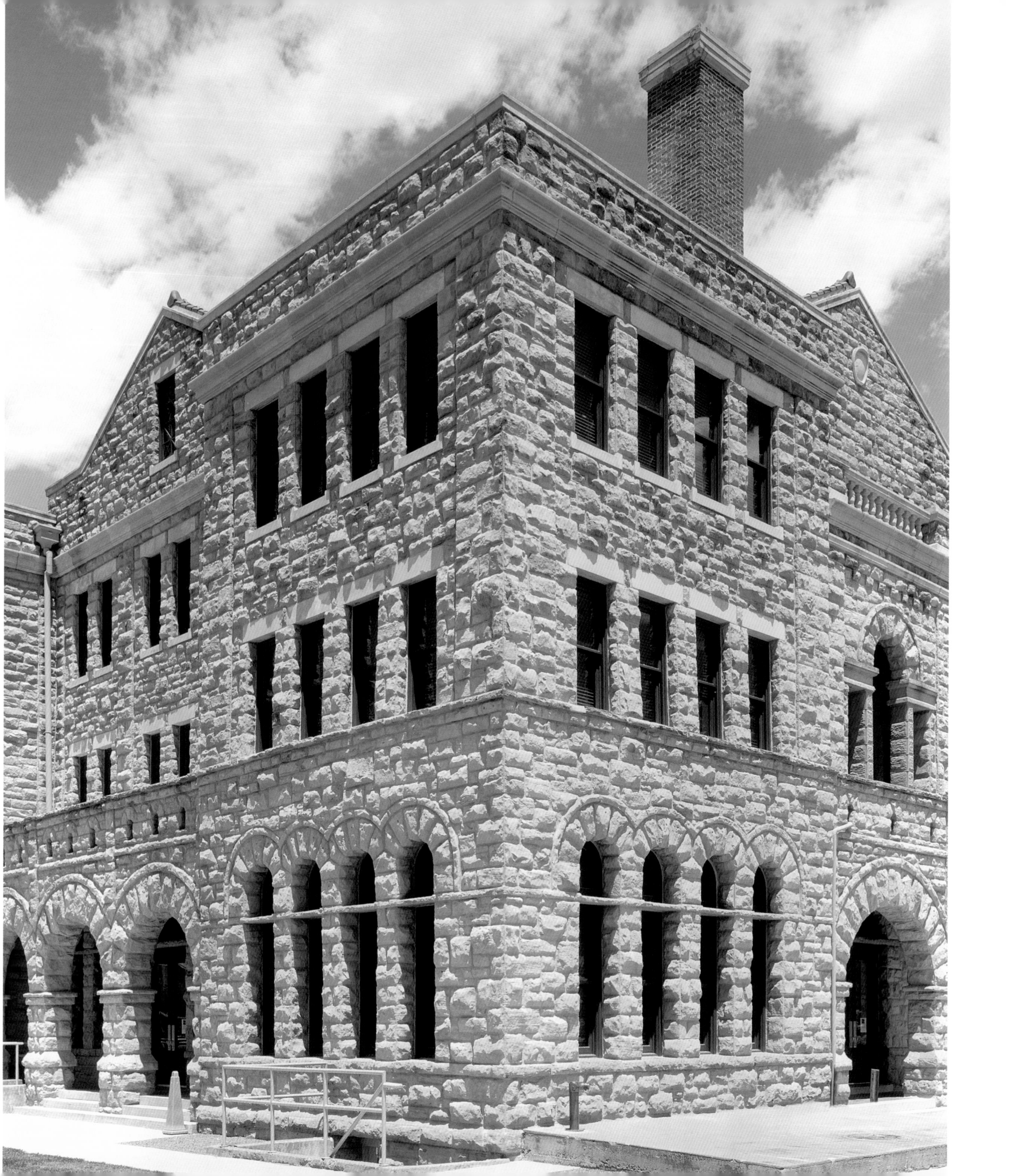

ARCHER COUNTY COURTHOUSE

Archer City. 1892/1926
Alonzo Newton Dawson (1892), Elmer George Withers (1926). Architects

When Archer County was created in 1880, C.B. Hutto, the town's founder, donated a one-story box house to serve as a courthouse. Ten years later it was replaced on the same site by a massive two-story temple of justice designed by Fort Worth architect Alonzo Dawson, who defeated twenty-five other architects for the prized commission. His masterpiece featured a large central tower with an octagonal dome and convex roofs that could be seen for miles. In 1926, county leaders commissioned another Fort Worth architect, Elmer Withers, to dramatically change the imposing structure, including removing the tower and roofs in order to add a third floor.[182]

This courthouse is made of locally quarried brown sandstone. It dominates the small town of Archer City today much as it did when it was completed in 1892. It was dramatically changed in 1926 and lost most of its monumental features, including a massive clock tower.

Preservationists at the Texas Historical Commission have decided to restore the building to its 1926 appearance, according to the plans of architect Elmer G. Withers. The building has undergone a major restoration as a result of the Texas Historic Courthouse Preservation Program. Wooden windows have been

installed that match the originals; the wooden floors, covered by layers of vinyl tile, have now been exposed; the low ceilings added in the 1960s were removed; and the district courtroom balcony has been restored. The 1926 courthouse was officially rededicated in 2005.

STEPHENS COUNTY COURTHOUSE

Breckenridge. 1926
David S. Castle. Architect

A t the end of World War I, Breckenridge was an isolated little West Texas town with a population of 500 citizens. There were, on any given weekend, more cattle in Breckenridge than people. And then in 1918, everything changed when wildcatters struck oil. It was a big discovery, bigger than anything anyone in Stephens County could imagine. In two years, the Breckenridge oil fields were producing fifty-million barrels a year. By the mid-1920s, the population had grown to thirty-thousand, with many new arrivals living in tents, and it was all about the oil. Derricks were everywhere—literally anywhere a well could be drilled, was drilled. Teachers, storeowners, cowboys—everyone tried their luck in the oil business.[183] A new courthouse was essential, and county leaders wanted the best their quick money could buy. By 1930, it was over. The economy spiraled downward into the Great Depression, and so did the inflated price of crude. The oil boom ended almost as fast as it had begun, but the magnificent courthouse remained.

This Classical Revival courthouse is the third for the county. The monumental four-story building by David Castle, with its engaged Corinthian columns, is a powerful statement. The inscription on the frieze reads: "Justice, Equality and Peace Administered Alike to All People."

Great historical lawgivers—Moses, Roman Emperor Titus, Byzantine Emperor Justinian and Babylonian King Hammurabi—grace the entablature above the second-floor windows. The rectangular building is constructed with gray limestone imported by rail from Indiana.

The central feature of this courthouse is the two-story row of ten engaged Corinthian columns, decorated with eagles and stars. This magnificent building is one of the most highly detailed courthouses of its era.

The previous courthouse, designed by James L. Flanders in 1883, occupied a corner of the square. Once the present courthouse was completed, the old building was demolished. A sandstone entry portal was saved and stands on the grounds as a memorial.

UVALDE COUNTY COURTHOUSE

Uvalde. 1927
Henry Truman Phelps. Architect

In the winter of 1883, John Nance Garner was a twenty-five-year-old new lawyer when he first arrived in Uvalde. He weighed 120 pounds and was almost penniless when he joined a two-man law firm with offices above a saloon on the courthouse square. Garner traveled the back roads of the nine county judicial circuits by buckboard and on horseback, sleeping on the ground at night. He earned a reputation around the courthouse as a skilled negotiator and for his ability to persuade juries. Garner was a tough, plain-spoken man who loved to drink and play poker with his friends who called him "Cactus Jack." When a vacancy opened in the office of county judge, Garner was appointed and served for three years. He was elected to the Texas Legislature in 1898, and in 1903, he was elected to the U.S. Congress. He served  in the House of Representatives for thirty years and was elected Speaker of the House by his colleagues. In 1932, Garner joined the ticket of Franklin D. Roosevelt and served two terms as vice president. Garner opposed Roosevelt's determination to serve a third term and was replaced by Henry Wallace. His long political career over, John Nance Garner returned to his home in Uvalde, a few blocks from the old courthouse square where he started.[184]

This limestone and brick building, designed by Henry T. Phelps, is similar to several Classical Revival courthouses built in Texas during the 1920s. This is the fifth courthouse for Uvalde County, which was founded in 1856. It replaced an aging 1890 courthouse. It features a substantial stone base with cast stone segmented arches at the entrances. The two-story Ionic columns are joined by a second-floor balustrade. A limestone entablature surrounds the building and supports the pediment with its distinctive clock.

Arched windows are placed on the first floor. The buff-colored brick exterior of the second and third floors is broken by the unadorned paired windows.

TOM GREEN COUNTY COURTHOUSE

San Angelo. 1928
Anton F. Korn. Architect

When Tom Green County was organized in 1873, the village of Ben Ficklin was named the county seat. The 600-acre hamlet was located at a Butterfield stage stopover and crossing of the South Concho River. Town leaders of San Angela had competed with Ben Ficklin citizens for the designation, but they lost by a handful of votes in every election. The issue seemed settled when a limestone courthouse was completed in 1882, but six months after its dedication, heavy rains swelled the Concho to more than forty feet out of its banks. The raging river drowned 65 people and destroyed everything in the town except the new courthouse. In a day, Ben Ficklin ceased to exist. The county seat was quickly moved to higher ground, and San Angela, later named San Angelo, became the permanent seat of government.[185]

This magnificent Classical Revival courthouse is more reminiscent of a federal building in Washington, D.C., than the wind-swept Edwards Plateau of west central Texas. The stone and brick building cost $200,000 to build.

Eighteen large Corinthian columns add dignity and importance to this monumental structure.

GRAY COUNTY COURTHOUSE

Pampa. 1929

William R. Kaufman. Architect

Gray County is located in the central part of the Panhandle on the eastern edge of the High Plains. In the late 1920s, the county enjoyed a surge of economic growth because of oil discoveries near Pampa, and local leaders voted to fund the construction of a new courthouse, fire station and city hall at the county square. W.R. Kaufman of Amarillo was commissioned to design all three civic buildings in the same style. They became known as "The Million Dollar Row."[186]

This courthouse is designed in a Beaux Arts style with Georgian ornamentation. The four-story steel frame building has an exterior of Indiana limestone and beige brick. Heavily rusticated limestone forms the base of the building and part of the first floor. Brick pilasters divide each facade into bays, and each pilaster is capped by a Corinthian capital.

The main entrance to the courthouse is signaled by the elimination of the limestone panels between the second and third floors. The entablature that encircles the building has a raised brick parapet with a limestone balustrade positioned over the outer bays. A cornice is positioned on an ornamented frieze.

The interior includes a courtroom with tall oak panels behind the judge's bench, golden oak benches and garnet-colored marble wainscoting in the foyers and halls.

The courthouse has never been significantly altered or remodeled. As a result, the historical integrity of the structure has remained secure. Working with state preservationists, county leaders have renovated and restored the courthouse, the second for Gray County. It was officially rededicated in 2003.

TEXAS MODERNE

In 1936, The Texas Centennial Exposition opened on the expansive State Fair Grounds surrounding the Cotton Bowl in Dallas. The purpose of the widely publicized year long event was to celebrate the one hundred year anniversary of Texas Independence and to highlight the economic, social and cultural progress of the country's largest state. The famed sculptor, Pompeo Coppini, designed statues of famous Texans in a Hall of Heroes. The exhibition was visited by President Franklin Roosevelt, movie stars and national celebrities, such as Gene Autry and Amelia Earhart. It was enormously successful, attracting more than six million people, and in every sense a celebration of the state's status as a national leader in agriculture, industry, technology and the arts.[187] A consortium of the leading architects and designers in Texas were commissioned under the leadership of noted architect George Dahl to design several of the public buildings that would hold the exhibits. Their work represents some of the very best examples of modernistic design in Texas during the 1930s.[188]

At the start of a new decade, American taste and architecture took a historic turn, and Texas was at the forefront. International styles were rapidly changing with a new vocabulary of modernistic design. Sleek public buildings across Texas were being designed during the 1930s by a new generation of creative, skilled architects that would reflect these changes and become an important break from past traditions.

Many of the most important modernistic styles that are so identified with the late 1920s and 1930s were first introduced at major international expositions, which were ideal to display creative design concepts for a new age of architecture. In 1925, the landmark Exposition des Arts Decoratifs et Industrielles Modernes held in Paris solidified the importance and popularity of Art Deco and Moderne in the world of architecture. The Century of Progress Exposition of 1933–1934 in Chicago, the Texas Centennial Exposition in 1936 and the New York World's Fair of 1939–1940 were reflections of a movement that actually commenced in Germany, France and Belgium in the mid-1920s and was firmly in place across America in the early years of the 1930s. These styles were significantly different from previous decades, and while their roots were European, the use of Moderne and Art Deco styles in the United States were uniquely American.[189]

These crisp streamlined Moderne buildings, with their Art Deco geometric patterns, long forms and curved surfaces, expressed the technological and scientific advances of the period. Many contemporary designs of the Great Depression, especially for courthouses, were more austere than their predecessors, as well as more practical and utilitarian. Public buildings of the decade were designed to function efficiently and fit the harsh economic restraints of the Great Depression. This was the age of the machine, and building design was changing as rapidly as the shape of automobiles and airplanes.[190]

These new architectural approaches fit the changing needs of county governments. As populations grew in numbers, local leaders needed more utilitarian and spatial buildings. During the 1920s, the population of Texas grew by more than one million people, a gain of almost 25 percent.[191] Efficiency and order were important standards as architectural firms of the period competed for commissions, and modernistic modes of design were perfectly suited for the governmental buildings of the decade. New courthouses exhibited smooth streamlined shapes, flat roofs and

a moderation of ornamentation. The Art Deco styles, with asymmetrical patterning and unbroken lines, that were highly popular in Europe, were translated into the designs of county courthouses in a much more modest and formal manner, befitting the solemn purpose of government. The use of decorative details, even though they might be sparse, gave Texas architects an opportunity to highlight the regional culture and historical heritage of a community. The 1932 courthouse in Potter County was adorned with cowboys and Indians, and a relief on the Brazoria County Courthouse of 1939 featured its burgeoning chemical and oil industry.

Advances in the use of basic building materials, such as concrete and steel, gave architects and contractors more construction options. In addition, the rapid development of mechanical and technological features, such as air conditioning and improved plumbing systems, made large public buildings more efficient and comfortable.[192]

The Great Depression caused enormous financial and social damage to Texans. On October 29, 1929, the crash of the stock market sent the country into a devastating economic tailspin. In 1930, national unemployment rose to 4 million, 8 million in 1931 and 12 million in 1932. Almost one out of every four workers in America was unemployed.[193] By 1932, approximately 15 percent of Texans were out of work, and the number of unemployed soared to almost 400,000.[194] In 1934, a severe drought devastated agricultural production in the state, adding to the despair and hardship. In 1928, Texans had voted overwhelmingly for the Republican candidate for the presidency, Herbert Hoover. Texans quickly changed their loyalties four years later and rewarded the Democratic nominee, Franklin Delano Roosevelt and his vice presidential nominee, Congressman John Nance Garner of Uvalde, with almost ninety percent of their vote.[195]

During the early months of the new administration, the president and the Congress moved quickly to respond to a worsening economic crisis. By the mid-1930s, the federally funded programs of the New Deal began pushing massive amounts of financial resources into the state for jobs, and generous subsidies for the construction of public works, including new courthouses.[196] By 1935, more than 20 percent of Texans were receiving federal aid.[197] Between 1933 and 1939, the Public Works Administration was responsible for 65 percent of the nation's courthouses and city halls.[198] Between 1929 and the commencement of World War II in 1941, approximately fifty courthouses were either built or remodeled in Texas, and most of them were in part federally financed through the Public Works Administration and the Works Progress Administration.

The projects meant construction jobs at a time when there was little work in the private sector. The PWA and the WPA gave struggling architects and contractors business opportunities and the chance to test new contemporary designs and construction techniques. In most instances, the architects chosen by the PWA were chosen by their reputation and portfolio of previous works, which afforded many local architects commissions for courthouses. Most importantly, the PWA did not dictate the design, specifications, construction materials or the character of any federally funded projects.[199] This allowed local political leaders great discretion in making decisions based on their county's specific needs and considerations. Regional PWA offices across the country administered the program, which allowed federal officials to respond to a region's special requirements, such as climate considerations and the availability of various building materials. In addition, transferring the decision-making out of Washington was reflected in the regional symbolism and decoration of many public structures. As importantly, the procedures encouraged architects to be creative and innovative in their designs, and in many instances, the result was sensational.

A few communities in Texas during the decade experienced an economic boom because of significant oil and gas discoveries and built new courthouses that reflected their prosperity. In 1931, new oil discoveries in Gregg County increased the population in a few weeks from 16,000 to more than 100,000 citizens. By 1935, the county's bank deposits had climbed from a modest $500,000 to more than $10 million.[200]

Gregg County and other oil-rich counties like Potter, Jefferson and Midland built expansive courthouses between 1930 and 1932. Most Texas counties, however, relied at least in part on the federal government to provide architectural and construction funds for new courthouses.

Hard times demanded a different response from government, and many elegant and decorative public buildings of the past seemed out of date and inefficient. A new generation of Texas architects responded. The prolific Wichita Falls firm of Voelker & Dixon designed nine county courthouses during this period. Fred C. Stone and his partner A. Basin; Travis Broesche of Houston; and the firm of Townes, Lightfoot & Funk all would make their mark on the decade. One of the most successful architectural firms of the era, Page Brothers, would design an outstanding courthouse for Travis County. These

professionals had more formal education and training than their predecessors, and with the expansion of information and ideas, they were on the cutting edge of new designs.

The county courthouses of Texas that were built during the 1930s are symbolic of their time and befitted the Texans who worked within their walls. The role of local government and the mandate of county officeholders shifted to address a rapidly deteriorating economy and an anxious constituency, one that was increasingly reliant on the services of government.

Moderne governmental buildings had less ornamentation than their predecessors, and they were not as monumental. They were designed to be efficient. Their clean simplicity and smooth finishes were a perfect architectural response to the demands of the era. They are important historical edifices on their own terms and lasting architectural achievements.

EASTLAND COUNTY

EASTLAND COUNTY COURTHOUSE

Eastland. 1928
Otto H. Lang. Architect

"Old Rip" was the name given to a horned toad that was placed in the cornerstone during the dedication of the new courthouse in 1897. When the courthouse was replaced in 1928 and a new building was dedicated, the stone was ceremoniously reopened by county leaders on the courthouse grounds, and "Old Rip" was lifted out alive. True or not, "Old Rip" brought nationwide publicity to Eastland. With local dignitaries, he toured the country and met with President Calvin Coolidge in the White House. After his return, he was stricken with pneumonia and died. He was placed in a marble and glass box and remains on public display in the county courthouse. A marker is dedicated to "Old Rip" on the courthouse steps.[201]

This Moderne building with Art Deco features was one of the first governmental buildings of its kind in the state. Constructed of beige bricks and smooth terra cotta, the motif would become almost a standard approach to courthouse design in the early 1930s.

This centrally massed edifice with its stacked cubes and rising central block would become a common denominator of the era's courthouses.

Large eagles and shields are carved into the corners of smooth stone.

COTTLE COUNTY COURTHOUSE

Paducah. 1930
Voelcker and Dixon. Architects

Cottle County was organized in January of 1892. The town of Paducah, located in the county's center along the banks of Salt Creek, was chosen as the county seat. One of the first official actions of newly elected County Judge L.L. Doolen was to sign a court order awarding "a bounty to be paid on the scalps of lobo wolves, panthers, Mexican lions and prairie dogs, these animals having become a nuisance to the people."[202]

Built in 1930 at a cost of $150,000, this four-story courthouse is a fine example of the Moderne style with its Art Deco features. The architectural firm of Voelcker and Dixon was one of the state's most successful designers of this popular mode of design.

The two principal facades with their stepped pavilions have arched entryways flanked by imposing buttresses. The Goddesses of Liberty and Justice stand tall against the central block of the building. Impressive winged eagles rest on the corners of this brick and stone centrally massed edifice. This is the county's third courthouse. The inscription high above the entrance reads: "To No One Will We Sell Deny or Delay Justice."

Soon after the new courthouse was built, the economic hardships of the Great Depression in a severe drought known as the Dust Bowl devastated those who lived on the arid prairies of

northwest Texas. Community leaders planted a large vegetable garden on the courthouse square to provide free food for the citizens of Paducah. During the decade, more than twenty percent of the county's residents moved away.[203]

MOORE COUNTY COURTHOUSE

Dumas. 1930
Barry and Hatch. Architects

In 1892, when the first courthouse was built for the new county, the population was 167, counting the cowboys who worked for the big ranches. I.W. Foreman worked on the courthouse: "After completion of the building, it was used by all the county. Not only was it the seat of government, but it served as a dance hall, camping ground for freighters and at one time, the hotel of the town moved in. The first church in Dumas was denied the privilege of meeting in the courthouse, however, because it might burn down."[204]

This decorative Moderne courthouse features a balanced row of beige-colored brick pilasters topped with Art Deco designs of carved terra cotta stone. Four tall Statues of Justice guard the courthouse, and eagles decorate the corners of the building. The main entrance is entered through a low arcaded loggia of smooth stone. Between two of the statues appears the inscription: "Justice Equity and Peace Administered Alike to All People."

TRAVIS COUNTY COURTHOUSE

Austin. 1930

Page Brothers. Architects

The second president of the Republic of Texas, Mirabeau B. Lamar, played an active role in the planning of the capital of the new republic. Raised in Georgia, Lamar was familiar with carefully planned towns like Savannah, and town squares were at the heart of his vision for the city. Austin would have four public squares, in addition to the land overlooking the town that was set aside for the Capitol building. The first county courthouse for Travis County was positioned near a square overlooking the Colorado River, and the second stood across the street from the Capitol grounds. The present courthouse would be built adjacent to one of the satellite squares, underscoring its secondary role in the capital city.[205]

Designed by Austin architects Charles and Louis Page, this large courthouse is an excellent example of a PWA Moderne government building. It was completed in 1930 at a cost of $750,000. Decorative features enhance the powerful statement of the building's purpose. Like many courthouses of the period, the top floor was set back to hide the county jail. A large disproportionate addition designed by the Page family firm was added in 1957, and the building was expanded again in 1962.

The building's interior originally enjoyed distinctive Art Deco features, including the judges' benches and a shoeshine stand. Periodic remodeling has taken its toll on the interior's refinements.

The exterior walls of the structure are made of shell-limestone quarried near Austin, with Art Deco ornamentation. Cast metal panels are placed between the tall, vertical windows.

LIBERTY COUNTY COURTHOUSE

Liberty. 1931
Corneil G. Curtis and A.E. Thomas. Architects

The town of Liberty was established in 1831 by the Mexican government. It is one of the oldest cities in Texas, and Liberty County was one of the first counties of the Republic of Texas. When Sam Houston first arrived in Texas, he opened a law office in Liberty and practiced in the rough-hewn log courthouse on the courthouse square. With his law partner, Houston purchased almost thirty-thousand acres of land in the area.[206] Seven courthouses have now occupied the site.

Corneil G. Curtis of Houston was the primary architect of this well-proportioned Moderne courthouse, completed in 1931. Four entrances connected with axial corridors divide each floor into quadrants. The exterior of the two-story building is made of cream-colored limestone with dark painted steel windows framed by pilasters. Low relief sculptural panels of pine trees, oil derricks, water lilies and Longhorns decorate the edifice. Winged governmental shields and eagles symbolize the building's public purpose. A large stone-paneled entablature caps the building.

POTTER COUNTY COURTHOUSE

Amarillo. 1931
Townes, Lightfoot & Funk. Architects

By the late 1800s, major cattle drives were no longer profitable. The rangeland was laced with fencing, and cutting barbed wire was a crime.[207] The dominance of powerful ranching interests brought a sense of order to the Texas Panhandle. In 1887, the big ranches held one of the last great roundups that included 200,000 head of cattle and encompassed four-million acres of land. But it was the coming of the railroads that changed the High Plains. Potter County was organized in 1887, and once the railroad entered the sleepy little cowtown near the head of Amarillo Creek, it was chosen as the county seat. By 1895, the big herds were driven to stockyards near the rail lines, and Amarillo became the largest cattle shipping center in the world.[208]

The third courthouse for Potter County is one of the best architectural examples of the period.[209] This centrally massed structure is a beautifully proportioned Moderne building clad in terra cotta stone. The main entrance features a tripartite arcaded loggia. The vertical emphasis of the structure is accomplished by piers and stepped massing.

Bas-relief panels above the entry and top of the central tower feature regional symbols such as a stately Native American and a pioneer on the building's front facade. Cast-aluminum Longhorns adorn two entrances. The entrance pavilions are decorated with blooming cacti prevalent in the Panhandle.

The Texas Historical Commission has authorized funding of preliminary plans for the possible preservation and restoration of this courthouse.

JEFFERSON COUNTY COURTHOUSE

Beaumont. 1932

Fred C. Stone and A. Babin. Architects

On the morning of January 10, 1901, one-armed Patillo Higgens was trying once again to get out of debt. He had gambled everything on the theory that oil could be found under a salt dome. Higgens convinced Anthony Lucas, one of the few engineers in the country who agreed with him, to keep drilling south of the sleepy little town of Beaumont in a field he named Spindletop. Lucas had joined Higgens after reading an advertisement in a trade journal. Their enterprise was out of money, and no one believed their theories. When the well erupted, it sounded like cannon shot and then came a geyser of oil, towering more than one-hundred feet in the air.[210] Almost overnight, Beaumont became the most important oil center in the country. The Spindletop field produced more oil in one day than the rest of the world combined.[211]

The fourth courthouse for Jefferson County is unique because it is the only skyscraper county courthouse in the state. Its central tower soars fourteen stories, a height that is much more pronounced because of the flat Coastal Plain that surrounds the county seat of Beaumont. This Moderne style building resembles a highly popular design for commercial buildings of the period, and is comparable to the state capitol of neighboring Louisiana. Both buildings were under construction at the same time. By 1930, oil and gas discoveries in East Texas, a burgeoning chemical industry and a deepwater port combined to give Beaumont an economic surge, as most of the state suffered through a growing economic depression.

The steel frame building is constructed of cream-colored limestone and buff-colored bricks. The base is made of rough-finished Colorado greenstone. Carved into the limestone trim are eagles, garlands of wheat sheaves and ferns. Shields and flags also decorate the exterior. Limestone panels feature carvings of cowboys, farmers and oil field workers. These Art Deco details give the building dignity and distinguish it from the surrounding urban landscape.

A pyramidal roof is composed of panels decorated in tiles with a beacon light mounted on a metal tower that can be seen for miles. A poorly designed large, pink granite addition was added to one side of the original structure.

The interior spaces of this great building are well-preserved. Its marble halls and the large district and county courtrooms are in pristine condition, and may be the best examples of Art Deco decoration of any courthouse in the State.

YOUNG COUNTY COURTHOUSE

Graham. 1932
Withers and Thompson. Architects

In the early morning hours of February 25, 1915, Tom Cherryhomes stood guard at the old courthouse to protect the evidence that had persuaded a Young County grand jury to indict the former county judge, E.W. Fry, the county treasurer and the county clerk for forgery and embezzlement of county funds. When the four gunmen rushed the young man, he emptied his two pistols, badly wounding one of his attackers before he himself was mortally wounded. The gunmen retreated, and the seriously injured attacker was found the following day in the judge's home. Tom Cherryhomes died from his wounds.[212] County prosecutors believed that the judge was one of the killers and charged him with murder. When Judge Fry's trial was heard in the courthouse where he had presided, a jury of his peers, after hearing the evidence and deliberating for twenty-five minutes, found him not guilty.[213] At his second trial, a jury failed to reach a verdict on the charge of embezzling money from the county. The district attorney elected not to appeal the decision, and Judge Fry, who had been elected to the state Legislature, left the courthouse a free man.[214] Descendents of Tom Cherryhomes placed a small stone marker behind the courthouse honoring him for giving his life to protect the county records.

This seat of government is entered through a prominent arcaded loggia made of smooth limestone. The granite base of the building was quarried at nearby Marble Falls. The design of the building is similar to the Eastland County courthouse, with impressive eagles perched on the building's corners, emphasizing its purpose.

The excellent bas-relief carvings on the wall panels of pioneers, Native Americans and cowboys symbolize the region's history and western influences.

KNOX COUNTY COURTHOUSE

Benjamin. 1935
Voelcker and Dixon. Architects

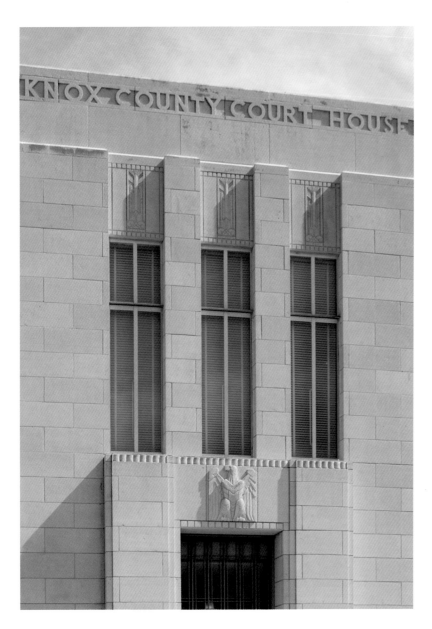

I n 1895, Father Joseph Reisdorff and a land developer named Hugo Herchenbach established a German Catholic colony in a valley along the Brazos River and named it Rhineland after a region in Germany. They built a small colony house, set aside lots for Catholic settlers and sent out circulars advertising their new town. They came by wagon, one family at a time, to the isolated little settlement. Mail was delivered by horseback twice a week. Within two years, a cotton gin, a blacksmith shop and a gristmill were built, and in 1897, the Lone Star Band of Rhineland was formed. Rhineland survived and still exists today in Knox County with a population of almost 200 citizens.[215]

Located in the Rolling Plains region of northwest central Texas, Knox County was formed by the Texas Legislature in 1858. Because of a scarce population, the county was not organized until 1886. The county seat is named after the son of the town's founder. This Moderne structure by Voelcker & Dixon is the county's third courthouse.

Primarily funded with federal relief funds, this courthouse was constructed with a reinforced concrete structural frame. The

vertical windows are framed by pilasters. The second and third floors are divided by cast metal panels. Low relief carvings of eagles and farming scenes signal the role of government and the area's economy.

GUADALUPE COUNTY COURTHOUSE

Seguin. 1935
L.M. Wirtz. Architect

I n 1806, Juan Nepomuceno Seguin was born into a respected Tejano family of great wealth and influence in San Antonio. Like his father, the young man was committed to public service, becoming a lawyer, an alcalde and later mayor of San Antonio. His loyalties were not with Mexico, but with Texas, and his commitment to independence brought many Tejanos to the side of the Texians. Seguin was one of the defenders of the Alamo and survived only because he was sent to find reinforcements. Joining Sam Houston's army, he fought bravely at San Jacinto and was a true hero of the revolution. Almost as soon as hostilities ended, Anglo attitudes toward Tejanos hardened, and men like Seguin were treated harshly, losing their lands and political power. Falsely accused of treason, an embittered Seguin left Texas, resettled in Mexico and later fought in the Mexican-American War against the United States.[216]

This Moderne courthouse replaced an Italianate courthouse designed by Alfred Giles, which was similar in scale to his design for Wilson County. The older building was demolished to build

the present edifice, the third courthouse for Guadalupe County. The PWA-funded building is built with concrete, steel and smooth sandstone with modest ornamentation. A large central block is sided with two smaller wings.

WISDOM

GRAYSON COUNTY COURTHOUSE

Sherman. 1936
Voelcker and Dixon. Architects

Built in 1876, the elegant courthouse on the square was for years the central focus and pride of the people of Sherman. For a half-century, the stately old building held daily court proceedings in its large second-story district courtroom. On May 3, 1930, a black farm hand named George Hughes confessed to the brutal rape of a white woman and was indicted two days later. The trial was quickly scheduled to begin within a week. On the morning of the trial, Texas Rangers and local sheriff's deputies brought the chained defendant to the courthouse for his trial. A large mob had already formed, and as jury selection began, the angry crowd threw rocks at the courthouse. When the first witness took the stand, the mob stormed into the building and was turned back by the Rangers using tear gas. The rioters set the stately old courthouse on fire with dynamite and cut the hoses of the firemen as they tried to put out the roaring blaze. Firemen helped the women and children escape the second-floor courtroom by ladders. The hapless judge declared a recess and ordered a change of venue. It was too late. The building was gutted. The defendant was left in the courtroom with a bucket of water and died in the fire. His charred body was dragged through the streets of the town and then hanged from a

tree and burned. The rioters set fires in the black-owned business district, destroying most of the buildings. Governor Dan Moody sent two units of National Guardsmen to finally restore law and order.[217]

This fine Moderne building by Voelcker and Dixon is the third to occupy the courthouse square in Sherman. It is constructed of concrete and native limestone. Like most courthouses of the period, the jail facilities are included in the top floor, which is set back from the front facade and partially hidden from the ground level.

VAN ZANDT COUNTY COURTHOUSE

Canton. 1937

Voelcker and Dixon. Architects

In 1877, when fifty Texas Rangers boarded a special train in Dallas and raced fifty miles eastward toward Van Zandt County, the disputed election had already spiraled out of control. Judge C.M. Rains had counted most of the votes when he declared Wills Point the new county seat and ordered the court records, archives and furniture moved from Canton. Three-hundred heavily armed men were on the march to Wills Point to bring the records back. In Wills Point, citizens barricaded their small wooden frame courthouse with cotton bales and waited, while some one-hundred men formed a posse to meet the attack. When the Rangers arrived, cooler heads prevailed, and a truce was negotiated: no arrests by the lawmen in exchange for no violence until the judicial appeals were concluded. The following year, the Texas Supreme Court set aside the election results and ordered the records and furniture returned to Canton. The Wills Point War was over.[218]

Depression-era county politicians razed the previous courthouse designed by J. Riely Gordon to build this new building. Principally funded by the Public Works Administration at a cost of $142,000, the project provided construction jobs for many unemployed citizens in Canton. The eagle on the courthouse lawn was atop the previous structure.

Moderne and Art Deco details highlight the cast stone exterior walls. The vertical emphasis of the stepped massed structure was central to a series of public buildings designed by the Wichita Falls- and Houston-based firm of Voelcker and Dixon. It is the sixth courthouse for Van Zandt County.

WASHINGTON COUNTY COURTHOUSE

Brenham. 1939
Travis Broesche. Architect

Washington-on-the-Brazos is one of the most historic sites in Texas. It was in the town's blacksmith shop that members of the Revolutionary Convention wrote the Texas Declaration of Independence, and it served as one of the first capitals of the Republic.[219] In the early 1840s, business leaders built three steamboats to plow up the Brazos River from the Gulf of Mexico. They invested their economic future in the commerce of the muddy river.[220] When the owners of the Houston and Texas Central Railroad asked the businessmen to pay a bonus of $11,000 to ensure that their railroad would cross the Brazos at Washington and stop in the town, the business leaders refused. They were wrong. Their steamboat venture failed, and the rails were laid through the new town of Brenham, which soon became the county seat. Washington became a ghost town.[221]

The Depression-era courthouse for Washington County is an excellent example. Utilizing smooth straight lines, contrasting black marble and minimal ornamentation, Houston architect Travis Broesche captured the PWA ideal of economy and scale.

One of the few decorative features, the powerful eagle perched above the entrance defines the building's purpose.

COMANCHE COUNTY COURTHOUSE

Comanche. 1939

Wyatt C. Hedrick. Architect

I n 1939, the citizens lined the public square to witness the demolition of their old courthouse to make way for a new building. Fifty WPA workers razed the stately 1890 edifice, which featured a lofty four-sided clock tower. It was an elegant monument to justice and a powerful symbol to the people of Comanche County. Local artisans had crafted the plaster ceilings, and stonemasons brought limestone from a nearby quarry to complete the grand building.[222] Designed by Larmour and Watson, it was similar to their courthouse for Milam County, which was restored and is still in use today.[223]

Architect Wyatt C. Hedrick used rusticated stone to achieve an interesting departure from the common use of smooth sandstone and concrete. As in earlier eras, the stone was quarried locally. A pair of eagles guards the entrances. Comanche County has had four courthouses. This building was completed with substantial funding from the WPA and the issuance of local bonds.

The first courthouse for Comanche County was located in the small settlement of Cora. It was a double-room log cabin  with a dogtrot center hall. County leaders saved the building, and today it sits on the edge of the county square, one of the only extant log courthouses from the early days of Texas.

ROCKWALL COUNTY COURTHOUSE

Rockwall. 1940
Voelcker and Dixon. Architects

The Great Depression was devastating to the Texas economy, especially to those areas heavily dependent on agriculture. In Rockwall County, the smallest county in the state, unemployment was high. Fifteen percent of the available workers were with relief jobs or in search of work. The federal government kept the struggling county government from bankruptcy through the use of federal relief funds. The old 1893 courthouse was razed to make room for a new $100,000 structure with the PWA paying $25,000 of the cost and giving sixty men jobs.[224]

This is the last of the series of six Moderne designed courthouses by Voelcker and Dixon. This single massed edifice with a setback attic is dominated by the vertically banked windows separated by piers. In many courthouses of the period, the attic contained the county's incarceration facilities. There is little exterior ornamentation on this solid, but modest, courthouse, the third for Rockwall.

CHEROKEE COUNTY

CHEROKEE COUNTY COURTHOUSE

Rusk. 1941
Gill and Bennett. Architects

T he county square in Rusk has been the primary stage for political campaigns since the county was organized in 1846, when Sam Houston debated his political opponents in front of the first log courthouse. In 1871, Colonel William S. Herndon was nominated as the area's congressman. He marched to the square with two-hundred supporters behind a Kickapoo Indian band to rally the voters of East Texas to his candidacy. In 1891, the former newspaper editor and reform-minded attorney general of Texas, James Stephen Hogg, launched his campaign for governor on the courthouse grounds, speaking to three-thousand people for three straight hours.[225]

As in the Comanche County courthouse, the architect's combination of rough stone and Art Deco geometric designs on the Cherokee courthouse blended regional qualities to the Moderne building design.[226] Cherokee County has had five courthouses.

TEXAS COUNTIES &
COUNTY SEATS

THE GOLDEN AGE OF TEXAS COURTHOUSES

Gillespie—Fredericksburg—1881
Shackelford—Albany—1883
Lampasas—Lampasas—1883
Bell—Belton—1884
Wilson—Floresville—1884
Red River—Clarksville—1884
Shelby—Center—1885
Maverick—Eagle Pass—1885
Parker—Weatherford—1886
Concho—Paint Rock—1886
Presidio—Marfa—1886
Leon—Centerville—1886
Brewster—Alpine—1888
Wharton—Wharton—1889
Hill—Hillsboro—1890
Throckmorton—Throckmorton—1890
Hood—Granbury—1890
Fayette—La Grange—1891
Colorado—Columbus—1891
Edwards—Rocksprings—1891
Donley—Clarendon—1891
Dallas—Dallas—1891
Sutton—Sonora—1891
Victoria—Victoria—1892
Erath—Stephenville—1892
Milam—Cameron—1892
Llano—Llano—1892
Grimes—Anderson—1894
Caldwell—Lockhart—1894
Goliad—Goliad—1894
Gonzales—Gonzales—1894
Somervell—Glen Rose—1894
Hopkins—Sulphur Springs—1894
Tarrant—Fort Worth—1895

Denton—Denton—1896
Ellis—Waxahachie—1896
Wise—Decatur—1896
Lavaca—Hallettsville—1897
DeWitt—Cuero—1897
Bexar—San Antonio—1897
Coryell—Gatesville—1897
Lee—Giddings—1897
Comal—New Braunfels—1898
McCulloch—Brady—1899
Irion—Sherwood—1901
Crockett—Ozona—1902

A NEW CENTURY

Harrison—Marshall—1900
McLennan—Waco—1902
Navarro—Corsicana—1905
Hartley—Channing—1906
Fort Bend—Richmond—1908
Hays—San Marcos—1908
Webb—Laredo—1909
Mason—Mason—1909
Harris—Houston—1910
Jeff Davis—Fort Davis—1910
Jones—Anson—1910
Cooke—Gainesville—1911
Williamson—Georgetown—1911
San Saba—San Saba—1911
Atascosa—Jourdanton—1912
Cameron—Brownsville—1912
Franklin—Mount Vernon—1912
Bee—Beeville—1912
Henderson—Athens—1913
Johnson—Cleburne—1913
Anderson—Palestine—1914

Kleberg—Kingsville—1914
Brooks—Falfurrias—1914
Nueces—Corpus Christi—1914
Trinity—Groveton—1914
Val Verde—Del Rio—1887/1915
Blanco—Johnson City—1916
Lamar—Paris—1917
Freestone—Fairfield—1919
Hudspeth—Sierra Blanca—1920
Dallam—Dalhart—1923
Schleicher—Eldorado—1924
Wheeler—Wheeler—1925
Archer—Archer City—1892/1926
Stephens—Breckenridge—1926
Uvalde—Uvalde—1927
Tom Green—San Angelo—1928
Gray—Pampa—1929

TEXAS MODERNE

Eastland—Eastland—1928
Cottle—Paducah—1930
Moore—Dumas—1930
Travis—Austin—1930
Liberty—Liberty—1931
Potter—Amarillo—1931
Jefferson—Beaumont—1932
Young—Graham—1932
Knox—Benjamin—1935
Guadalupe—Seguin—1935
Grayson—Sherman—1936
Van Zandt—Canton—1937
Washington—Brenham—1939
Comanche—Comanche—1939
Rockwall—Rockwall—1940
Cherokee—Rusk—1941

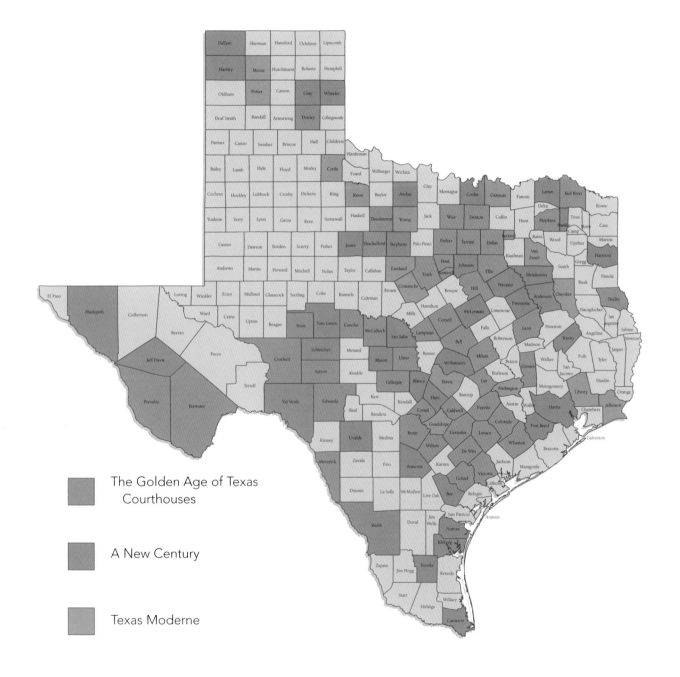

The Golden Age of Texas
Courthouses

A New Century

Texas Moderne

GLOSSARY OF ARCHITECTURAL TERMS

Arcade: a series of arches supported on piers or columns.

Arch: a curved masonry construction for spanning an opening; consists of a number of stones or bricks.

Architrave: the lowermost member of a Classical entablature, located below the frieze.

Ashlar: a squared or rectangular building stone.

Balcony: a railed or balustraded elevated platform projecting from the wall of a building.

Baluster: a number of closely spaced supports for a railing.

Balustrade: a railing with supporting balusters.

Base: the lowermost support of a beam or pier.

Battlement: a fortified parapet or cresting with alternating openings, used in the nineteenth century for decoration.

Beam: relatively long pieces of wood, stone or metal used as rigid members or parts of structures.

Belt course: a horizontal band of molding that extends across the facade of a building, its band broken by windows or other architectural features.

Billet: a decorative band created by using a checkerboard pattern with cubes, cylinders or prisms.

Brace: anything that holds parts of a structure together or in place.

Bracket: a support projecting from a wall to support the weight of a cornice or other projecting part of a building.

Buttress: an external support or prop built to steady a structure wall.

Capital: the uppermost portion of a column or pillar.

Colonnade: a series of regularly placed columns supporting an entablature.

Console: an ornamental supporting bracket.

Corbel: a bracket, usually made of brick or stone, that projects from a wall and is used for support.

Corinthian order: a Classical type of column and entablature that is usually decorative, incorporating acanthus leaves.

Cornerstone: a stone uniting two masonry walls at an intersection.

Cornice: a projecting, continuous, prominent horizontal feature.

Crenellation: a notch or indentation in a wall.

Cresting: a decorative balustrade usually designed to decorate a roof.

Cruciform: cross-shaped.

Cupola: a small structure on a dome, tower or roof.

Dentil: a decorative band of small rectangular blocks, especially under a cornice.

Doric order: a Classical type of architecture noted for its simplicity.

Dormer: a window set vertically, projecting from a sloping roof.

Double-hung window: a window with two vertically sliding sashes.

Drum: a cylindrical form that supports a cupola or dome.

Engaged column: a column that is attached in part to a building.

Entablature: a horizontal part in Classical architecture, usually resting above a column that is composed of a cornice and a frieze.

Facade: the exterior face of a building, usually the front.

Finial: an ornament or detail placed at the high point of a structure, such as a roof or tower.

Frieze: the part of a Classical entablature between the architrave and the cornice.

Gable: the triangular portion of the front or the end of a building enclosed by a pitched roof.

Garland: a decorative wreath.

Hipped roof: a roof with sloping ends or sides.

Ionic order: a Classical style of architecture that features a volute as a prominent part of the capital.

Keystone: a wedge-shaped piece at the summit of an arch.

Lantern: a tall, generally open fixture on a dome or tower for light or ventilation.

Lintel: a horizontal member, such as a beam, supporting the weight above an opening.

Loggia: a gallery or arcade open on at least one side.

Mansard roof: a roof with two slopes on all sides, the lower slope steeper than the upper slope.

Molding: a long narrow strip that projects from a wall, used for ornamental or functional purposes.

Newel: a primary post at the top or bottom of a stairway that supports a handrail.

Parapet: a low wall or railing that rises above the roof of a structure.

Pavilion: a major projecting part of a building's facade.

Pedestal: a support for a column, statue or pilaster.

Pediment: a low gable or gable-like feature usually trimmed with cornices, sometimes filled with relief sculpture.

Pendant: a suspended ornamental feature in the interior of a building.

Pilaster: an upright rectangular feature projecting from a wall, sometimes resembling a column.

Pinnacle: a decorative architectural feature rising above a roof, tower or buttress.

Pitch face: rough-faced quarried stones.

Polychromy: the decorative use of many colors.

Portico: a roofed porch-like structure, often at a building's entrance.

Quoin: an external solid block at the angle of a wall or corner of a building.

Reentrant angle: walls meeting at right angles pointing inward to the structure.

Reinforced concrete: concrete reinforced with metal bars.

Roman or round arch: a round semi-circular arch.

Rusticated: stonework having a rough or irregular surface.

Segmental arch: a shallow arch with a curvature that is less than a semi-circle.

Slate: roofing made from construction materials, usually quarried stone.

Spire: the upper part of a steeple or a tall pointed pyramidal roof.

Stilted arch: a segmental arch with a short vertical section below each end.

Stringcourse: a continuous horizontal molding on a building's exterior.

Terra cotta: building material made of fired clay, usually brownish-orange in color.

Terrazzo: mosaic flooring made of pieces of marble set in mortar and polished.

Turret: a tower-like ornamental structure attached to a larger structure.

Visage: a face or appearance of a face, sometimes used in architectural ornamentation.

Wainscoting: An interior wall covering that usually rises only a few feet from the floor.

Water table: exterior molding a few feet above the ground, projecting, so as to throw off water.

BIBLIOGRAPHY

Editor's note: Footnotes identified at the end of each entry.

Anderson, Jr., Garland. "Coryell County Courthouse." *Texas Architect* (February 1968): 24–25. 115

Angleton Times: August 3, 1923. 125

Barker, Eugene C., ed. *A History of Texas and Texans.* Chicago and New York: The American Historical Society, 1914. 8

Barnstone, Howard. *The Galveston That Was.* New York: Macmillan, 1966. College Station, TX: Texas A&M University Press, 1999. 33

Barr, Michael. "A Comparative Examination of Federal Work Relief in Fredericksburg and Gillespie County." *Southwestern Historical Quarterly* 96 (January 1993): 365–391. 194, 197

Batte, Lelia M. *History of Milam County, Texas.* San Antonio, TX: The Naylor Company, 1956. 84

Bennett, Carmen Taylor. *Our Roots Grow Deep: A History of Cottle County.* Floydada, TX: Blanco Offset Printing, Inc., 1970. 202, 203

Bernstein, Patricia. *The First Waco Horror: The Lynching of Jesse Washington and the Rise of the NAACP.* College Station, TX: Texas A&M University Press, 2005. 134

Block, Viola. *A History of Johnson County and Surrounding Areas.* Waco, TX: Texian Press, 1970. 161

Boethel, Paul C. *Sand in Your Craw.* Austin,TX: Von Boeckmann-Jones, 1959. 109

Braudaway, Douglas. *Del Rio: Queen City of the Rio Grande.* Charleston, SC: Arcadia Publishing, 2002. 171

Breeze, Carla. *Pueblo Deco.* New York, NY: Rizzoli International Publications, 1990. 199, 209

Breisch, Kenneth A. "The Richardson Interlude in Texas: A Quest for Meaning and Order at the End of the Nineteenth Century." *The Spirit of H.H. Richardson on the Midland Prairies.* Ed. Paul Clifford Larson with Susan M. Brown. Ames, IA: Iowa State University Press, 1972. 86–105. 39

Browder, Virginia. *Donley County Land O' Promise.* Wichita Falls, TX: Nortex, 1975. 77

Brown, Charles, ed. *The History of Franklin County, 1874–1964.* Mount Vernon, TX: Key Club, District T.F.W.C., 1964. 157

Broyles, William. "The Last Empire." *Texas Monthly* Oct 1980: 153–278. 164

Caldwell, Shirley, Bob Green, and Reilly Nail. *For 500 Years: The Shackelford County Courthouse.* Albany, TX: Bright Sky Press, 2001. 46

Caro, Robert A. *The Years of Lyndon Johnson: Path to Power.* New York, NY: Alfred A. Knopf, Inc., 1982. 140,173

—-. *The Years of Lyndon Johnson: Means of Ascent.* New York, NY: Alfred A. Knopf, Inc., 1990. 54

Clark, James A. and Michael T. Halbouty. *Spindletop.* Houston, TX: Gulf Publishing Company, 2000. 210, 211

Clark, L.D., ed. *Civil War Recollections of James Lemuel Clark.* College Station, TX: Texas A&M University Press, 1984. 150

Cleburne Morning Review: April 16, 1912. 160

Cocke, Stephanie Hetos. "Atlee B. and Robert M. Ayres." *Texas Architect* Nov.–Dec. 1989: 42. 130

Colorado County Historical Commission. *Colorado County Chronicles from the Beginning to 1923.* Austin, TX: Nortex, 1986. 72

Connor, Seymour V. "The Evolution of County Government in the Republic of Texas." *Southwestern Historical Quarterly* 55 (October 1951): 163–200. 9

Coote, Robert James. *The Eclectic Odyssey of Atlee B. Ayres, Architect.* College Station, TX: Texas A&M University Press, 2001. 130

Council, John. "Secret Stairway for Jurists Who Made Unpopular Rulings." *Texas Lawyer* 16 Jan, 2006: 8–9. 98

"Courthouse in Alpine Completed in 1887 but no one seems to know who built it." *Alpine Avalanche.* 14 Sept. 1951: 62. 65

"Courthouse Restored!!!" *Hillsboro Reporter.* 22 April 1999. 68

Cox, Edwin T. *History of Eastland County, Texas.* San Antonio, TX: Naylor, 1950. 201

Crawford, Leta. *A History of Irion County, Texas.* Waco, TX: Texian Press, 1966. 122

Crockett County Historical Society. *A History of Crockett County.* San Angelo, TX: Anchor Publishing Company, 1976. 124

Davis, William C. *Lone Star Rising.* New York, NY: Free Press, 2004. 216

De Bruhl, Marshall. *Sword of San Jacinto: A Life of Sam Houston.* New York, NY: Random House, 1993. 133, 206

DeLeon, Arnoldo. *They Called Them Greasers: Anglo Attitudes Toward Mexicans in Texas, 1821–1900.* Austin, TX: University of Texas Press, 1983. 73, 93

DeWitt County Historical Commission. *The History of DeWitt County, Texas.* Dallas, TX: Curtis Media Corporation, 1991. 111

Didear, Hedwig Krell. *A History of Karnes County and Old Helena.* Austin, TX: San Felipe Press, 1969. 4

Dietrich, Wilfred O. *The Blazing Story of Washington County.* Brenham, TX: Brenham Banner-Press, 1950; rev. ed., Wichita Falls, TX: Nortex Offset Publications, 1973. 219, 220, 221

Duke, Cordia Sloan and Joe B. Franz. *6,000 Miles of Fence: Life on the XIT Ranch of Texas.* Austin, TX: University of Texas Press, 1961. 137

Fairfield Recorder: April 29, 1993. 176

Faulk, J.J. *History of Henderson County.* Athens, TX: Athens Review Printing Co., 1929. 159

Fehrenbach, T.R. *Lone Star: A History of Texas and the Texans.* New York, NY: American Legacy Press, 1983. 3, 172

Fort Worth Gazette: April 22, 1893. 100

Fox, Stephen. "Profile: Nichols J. Clayton, Architect." *Texas Architect* July–Aug. 1976: 51–52. 34, 35, 36

Freeman, Douglas Southall. *R.E. Lee: A Biography.* New York, NY: Charles Scribner's Sons, 1936. 69

Gambrell, Herbert Pickens. *Anson Jones: The Last President of Texas.* Garden City, NY: Doubleday, 1948. 149

Gebhard, David. "The Moderne in the U.S., 1920–1941." *Architecture Association Quarterly* April 1970: 4–20. 189

George, Mary C.H. *Alfred Giles: An English Architect in Texas and Mexico.* San Antonio, TX: Trinity University Press, 1972. 19, 43, 45

Goeldner, Paul. "Our Architectural Ancestors." *Texas Architect* July–Aug. 1974: 5–8. 113

Gonzalez, John. *Fort Worth Star-Telegram.* 20 Sept. 1994. 102

Goodnight, Charles. "The Panhandle's First Settlements." *Frontier Times* Dec. 1929: 113–16. 181

Graham Leader: February 25, 1915; April 23, 1915; July 2, 1915. 212, 213, 214

Gray County History Book Committee. *Gray County Heritage.* Dallas, TX: Taylor Publishing Company, 1985. 186

Gray, Mrs. R.D. *Early Days in Knox County.* New York, NY: Carlton Press, 1963. 215

Green, Stan. *The Rise and Fall of Rio Grande Settlements: A History of Webb County.* Laredo, TX: Border Studies Publishing, 1991. 142

Greif, Martin. *Depression Modern: The Thirties Style in America.* New York, NY: Universe Books, 1975. 190

Hall, Margaret Elizabeth. *A History of Van Zandt County.* Austin, TX: Jenkins Publishing Company, 1976. 18, 218

Hall, Martin Hardwick. *Sibley's New Mexico Campaign.* Albuquerque, NM: University of New Mexico Press, 2000. 175

Hallettsville Enterprise: April 27, 1987. 14

Hamilton, Nancy and the Lee County Historical Commission. *Images of America: Lee County, Texas.* Charleston, SC: Arcadia Publishing, 1999. 117

Hawkins, Edna Davis et al. *History of Ellis County, Texas.* Waco, TX: Texian Press, 1972. 106

Hendricks, Patricia D. and Becky Duval Reese. *A Century of Sculpture in Texas, 1889–1989.* Austin, TX: Huntington Art Gallery, University of Texas Press, 1991. 81

Henry, Jay C. *Architecture in Texas 1895–1945.* Austin, TX: University of Texas Press, 1993. 37, 120, 128, 129, 131, 132, 136, 168, 178, 188, 226

—. "The Richardson Romanesque in Texas: An Interpretation." *Texas Architect* March–April 1981: 52–59. 38, 82

Hitchcock, Henry-Russell. *The Architecture of H.H. Richardson and His Times.* Hamden, CT: Archon Books, 1961. 23

Holland, G.A. *History of Parker County and the Double Log Cabin.* Weatherford, TX: Weatherford Herald, 1931. 57

Hood County News: June 27, 1976. 70

Houston Chronicle: July 8, 1934. 145

Houston Daily Post: November 10, 1910; November 11, 1910. 74, 75

Hunter, Lillie Mae. *The Book of Years: A History of Dallam and Hartley Counties.* Hereford, TX: Pioneer Book Publishers Inc., 1969. 1, 138, 179

Irwin, Jack C. "Dallas County Courthouse." *Texas Architect* April 1968: 25–27. 78, 79

Jacobson, Lucy Miller and Mildred Bloys Nored. *Jeff Davis County, Texas.* Fort Davis, TX: Fort Davis Historical Society, 1993. 147, 148

James, Marquis. T*he Raven: A Biography of Sam Houston.* Indianapolis, IN: The Bobbs-Merrill Company, 1929. 20, 153

Jones, Walter E. *"History of Gregg County."* The State Book of Texas, Ed. Arthur Waldo Stickle. Austin, TX: The Bureau of Research and Publicity, 1937. 200

Key, Della Tyler. *In the Cattle Country: A History of Potter County 1887–1966.* Quanah, TX: Nortex, 1972. 208

Killen, Mrs. James C. and the Lee County Historical Survey Committee. *History of Lee County Texas.* Quanah, TX: Nortex Press, 1974. 116

Kostof, Spiro. A *History of Architecture: Settings and Rituals.* New York, NY: Oxford University Press, 1979. 24, 198

Laws of Texas 1822–1897. Compiled and arranged by H.P.N. Gammel. Austin, TX: Gammel Book Co., 1898. 17, 22, 127, 207

LeFevre, Hazie Davis. *Concho County History: 1858–1958.* Eden, TX: H.D. LeFevre, 1959. 59

London, G.D. "Nig." *Through the Years, A Collection of Cowboy Stories.* Comp. Elizabeth London, and Georgia London Keeter. [Throckmorton: n. p. c. 1996]. 12

Lotto, Frank. *Fayette County: Her History and Her People.* Schulenburg, TX: Sticker Steam Press, 1902. 71

Lowry, Bullitt. ed. and David Strother. comp. *Building the Denton County Courthouse, 1895–1897.* Denton, TX: Denton County Historical Commission, Terrill Wheeler Printing Company, 1987. 103, 104

Lynch, James D. *The Bench and Bar of Texas.* St. Louis, MO: Nixon-Jones Printing Co., 1885. 112

Madray, Mrs. IC *A History of Bee County.* Beeville, TX: Beeville Publishing Co., 1939. 158

Makovy, Ernie. *Fort Worth Star-Telegram.* 2 July 1992. 101

Man, Art. "Courthouse Burns!!!" *Hillsboro Reporter.* 7 Jan. 1993. 67,

Mears, Mildred Watkins. *Coryell County Scrapbook.* Gatesville, TX: Coryell County Museum Foundation, 1985. 114

Meister, Chris. "Alfred Giles vs. El Paso County: An Architect Defends His Reputation on the Texas Frontier, *Southwestern Historical Quarterly* 108 Oct. 2004: 181–209. 61

Meister, Maureen, ed. *H.H. Richardson: The Architect, His Peers, and Their Era.* Cambridge, MA: The MIT Press, 1999. 25

Metz, Leon Claire. *John Wesley Hardin: Dark Angel of Texas.* El Paso, TX: Mangan Books, 1996. 95

Middleton, John W. *History of the Regulators and Moderators and the Shelby County War in 1841 and 1842, in the Republic of Texas, with facts and incidents in the early history of the Republic and State, from 1837 to the annexation, together with incidents of frontier life and Indian troubles, and the war on the Reserve in Young County in 1857.* Fort Worth, TX: Loving Publishing Company, 1883. 133

Montejano, David. *Anglos and Mexicans in the Making of Texas, 1836–1986.* Austin, TX: University of Texas Press, 1987. 143, 156, 166

Morgan, Charles D. "The Comanche County Courthouse, 1890–1939." *Texas Architect* Dec. 1969: 18–21. 222

Moseley III, Laurie, ed. *Somervell County Centennial, 1875–1975.* Glen Rose, TX: Somervell County Centennial Association, 1975. 97

Murchison, William P. "Courthouses." *Navarro County History.* Corsicana, TX: Navarro County Historical Association, 1985. 135

Nance, Joseph Milton. *After San Jacinto, The Texas-Mexican Frontier, 1836–1841.* Austin, TX: University of Texas Press, 1963. 52, 167

Neville, A.W. *The History of Lamar County, Texas.* Paris, TX: The North Texas Publishing Company, 1937; rpt. 1986. 174

Newlin, Blanche. "The Courthouses and Jails of Schleicher County." *Schleicher County or Eighty Years of Development in Southwest Texas* (1930): 180

Neyland, James. *The Anderson County Courthouse: A History.* Palestine, TX: Anderson County Historical Commission, 1992. 162, 163

Odom, Susan. *The Grand Old Lady of Presidio County: An Architectural and Historical Narrative.* Austin, TX: Nortex Press, 2001. 60, 126

O'Gorman, James F. *Living Architecture: A Biography of H.H. Richardson.* New York, NY: Simon & Schuster, 1997. 26

O'Keefe, Ruth Jones. *Archer County Pioneers: A History of Archer County, Texas.* Hereford, TX: Pioneer Book Publishers, 1969. 182

O'Neal, Bill. *The Bloody Legacy of Pink Higgins: A Half Century of Violence in Texas.* Austin, TX: Eakin Press, 1999. 48

Patenaude, Lionel V. *Texans, Politics and the New Deal.* New York, NY: Garland Publishing Co., 1983. 195, 196

Peters, John O. and Margaret T. *Virginia's Historic Courthouses.* Charlottesville, VA: University of Virginia Press, 1995. 21

Pingenot, Ben E. *Historical Highlights of Eagle Pass and Maverick County.* Eagle Pass, TX: Eagle Pass Chamber of Commerce, Sparks Printing Co., 1971. 55

Polk, Stella Gibson. *Mason and Mason County: A History.* Austin, TX: The Pemberton Press, 1966. 144

Ragsdale, Kenneth B. *Centennial Series of the Association of Former Students, Texas A&M University, No. 23: The Year America Discovered Texas Centennial '36.* College Station: Texas A&M University Press, 1987. 187

Ramsay Jr., Jack C. *Thunder Beyond the Brazos: Mirabeau B. Lamar, a Biography.* Austin, TX: Eakin Press, 1984. 139

Roach, Hattie Joplin. *A History of Cherokee County Texas.* Dallas, TX: Southwest Press, 1934. 225

Robbins, Mary Alice. "Courthouse Renovations Make Proceedings Hard to Hear." *Texas Lawyer* 17 Oct. 2005: 6–7. 49

Robinson, Duncan W. *Judge Robert McAlpin Williamson.* Austin, TX: Texas State Historical Association, 1948. 151

Robinson, Willard B. *Gone From Texas: Our Lost Architectural Heritage.* College Station, TX: Texas A&M University Press, 1981. 32, 223

—-. *The People's Architecture: Texas Courthouses, Jails, and Municipal Buildings.* Austin, TX: The Texas State Historical Association, 1983. 2, 6, 7, 27, 28, 29, 30, 31, 47,121, 165, 192

—-. "The Public Square as a Determinant of Courthouse Form in Texas." *Southwestern Historical Quarterly* 75 (1971–1972): 339–372. 16

Rodnitzky, Jerry L. and Shirley R. *Jazz Age Boomtown.* College Station, TX: Texas A&M University Press, 1997. 183

San Angelo Standard-Times: October 19, 1974. 185

Sanders, Allison. *Houston Chronicle.* 10 May 1935. 89

Sansom, Andrew. *Texas Past: Enduring Legacy.* Austin, TX: University of Texas Press, 1997. 123

Schlesinger, Jr. Arthur M. *The Age of Roosevelt Volume: The Crisis of the Old Order.* Boston, MA: Houghton Mifflin Company, 1957. 193

Schultz, David. "Renovation of Old Red." *The Dallas County Chronicle. 2001, Vol. 29: 1.* 80

Scott, Zelma. *A History of Coryell County Texas.* College Station, TX: Texas A&M University Press, 1965. 114

Silverstein, Vivian. "The Law and James Riely Gordon." *Texas Bar Journal* Oct. 1982: 1306–09. 40, 41, 42

Simpson, Harold B. *Hood's Texas Brigade: Lee's Grenadier Guard.* Waco, TX: Texian Press, 1970. 62, 63

Smith, A. Morton. *The First 100 Years of Cooke County.* San Antonio, TX: Naylor Company, 1955. 150

SoRelle, James M. "The 'Waco Horror': The Lynching of Jesse Washington." *Southwestern Historical Quarterly* 86 (April 1983): 517–537. 134

Spellman, Paul N. *Captain John H. Rogers, Texas Ranger.* Denton, TX: University of North Texas Press, 2003. 170

Spiller, Wayne. *Handbook of McCulloch County History, Vol. 1.* Seagraves, TX: Pioneer Book Publishers, 1976. 119

State of Texas v. Joe Palmer, No. 9230, District Court of Grimes County, Texas, June Term, 1934. 88

Sutton County Historical Society. *Sutton County.* Sonora, TX: Sutton County Historical Society, 1979. 87

Tanner, Leon and Mary Kemp. *Boots to Briefcases*. Weatherford, TX: Nebo Valley Press, 2003. 58

The Alfred Giles Collection. Alexander Architectural Archive. Austin, TX: University of Texas at Austin General Library. 44

The Dallas Morning News: September 3, 1941. 224

The James Riely Gordon Collection. School of Architecture. Austin, TX: University of Texas at Austin Architectural Library.

Thomas, Myrna Tryon. *The Windswept Land: A History of Moore County, Texas*. Dumas, TX: Quarto Publishing, 1967. 204

Tietz, Susan and Amy Lambert. "Uncovering Buried Treasurers." *The Medallion* (January/February, 2005): 4–5. 53, 56

Timmons, Bascom N. *Garner of Texas*. New York, NY: Harper & Brothers, 1948. 184

Tyler, George W. *The History of Bell County*. San Antonio: TX: The Naylor Company, 1936. 50

Vandiver, Frank E. *Black Jack: The Life and Times of John J. Pershing*. College Station, TX: Texas A&M University Press, 1977. 85

Veselka, Robert E. *The Courthouse Square in Texas*. Austin, TX: University of Texas Press, 2000. 5, 10, 11, 13, 15, 205

Webb, Walter Prescott. *The Texas Rangers: A Century of Frontier Defense*. Austin, TX: University of Texas Press, 1980. 141, 154, 177

Welch, June Rayfield and J. Larry Nash. *The Texas Courthouse*. Dallas, TX: GLA Press, 1971. 76

Whisenhunt, Donald W. *The Depression Years in Texas: The Hoover Years*. New York, NY: Garland Publishing Co., 1983. 191

Williams, Annie Lee. *A History of Wharton County 1846–1961*. Austin, TX: Von Boeckmann-Jones, 1964. 66

Williams, Chester and Ethel Hander Geue, eds. *A New Land Beckoned: German Immigration to Texas, 1844–1847*. Waco, TX: Texian Press, 1966. 118

Williams, Kathy. *The Dallas Morning News*. 10 May 1990. 217

Wilson County Historical Association. *Wilson County Centennial*. Floresville, TX: Wilson County Historical Association, 1960. 51

Wise County Messenger: September 13, 1895. 110

UNPUBLISHED WORKS

Anderson, Jr., Garland Sadler. "The Courthouse Square: Six Case Studies in Texas: Evolution, Analysis and Projections." Master's thesis, University of Texas at Austin, 1968. 50, 96

"Atascosa County Centennial: 1856–1956." Atascosa County: TX: Atascosa County Centennial Association, 1956. 155

Bowles, Flora G. "A History of Trinity County, Texas, 1827 to 1928." Master's thesis, University of Texas, 1928; rpr., Groveton, TX: Groveton Independent School District, 1966. 169

"Brewster County, Texas and its Courthouses: February 2, 1887–February 2, 1999." Brewster County Historical Commission, 1999. 64

Butler, Gary. "Gonzales' Salerno Action Revisited." *T-Patch, 36th Division News*. Austin, TX: Texas Military Forces Museum, 2001.

http://www.kwanah.com/36division/tpatch/vn4/4408061a.htm. 146

Butler, Gary. "36 Division, World War I Period." Austin, TX: Texas Military Forces Museum, 2004.

http://www.kwanah.com/txmilmus/tnghist19htm 86

Ellis County Museum, Inc. Waxahachie, Texas, 2005.

http://www.rootsweb.com/~txecm/index.htm. 105, 107, 108

George, Carolyn Hollers. Memorandum to the Texas Historical Commission. Austin. 18 September 1998. 92, 94

LeFevre, Hazie. *Concho County History: 1858–1958*. Eden, Texas, 1959. 59

O'Banion, Maurine M. "The History of Caldwell County." Master's thesis, University of Texas at Austin, 1931. 90, 91

Scarbrough, Clara. *Courthouses of Williamson County*. Georgetown Heritage Society, Georgetown Chamber of Commerce, Williamson County. 152

Scott, Robert. "History of Erath County Courthouse." Dedication Program from the Recently Restored Erath County Courthouse and New Annex, 1988. 83

Texas Ranger Dispatch Magazine (Summer, 2004): http://www.texasranger.org/dispatch/12/hughes&Aten.htm. 55

INDEX